UNMUTED

UNMUTED

**Stories of
Courage and
Resilience**

from the **GenPRIDE Community**

UNMUTED: Stories of Courage and Resilience from the GenPRIDE Community

Copyright © 2020 by GenPRIDE

Library of Congress Control Number: 2020916182

Paperback ISBN: 978-1-7355735-0-2

Ebook ISBN: 978-1-7355735-1-9

FIRST EDITION

Written by: Irene Calvo, Shayla Marie, Jenny Robinson, Steven Knipp, Amy D. Rubin, Eric Pierre Carter, Greg Colucci, Chris Doelling, Nancy Kiefer, M. Ames, Kevin Charles Patz, Natalie Pascale Boisseau, Mary Edwards, and Hope Bless.

Developmental Editing and Writing Coaching by Ingrid Ricks

Published in the United States by GenPRIDE

genprideseattle.org

Cover & Book Design by All She Wrote Productions

allshewroteproductions.com

In Dedication to Kevin Charles Patz

FEBRUARY 3, 1956 - MARCH 22, 2020

THE KEVIN I met in 1982 had recently moved to Seattle from San Francisco. He had a federal arrest record for protesting against nuclear weapons at Bangor Naval Station on Hood Canal, a holdover from his Jesuit days when he worked in a soup kitchen. He was a would-be flight attendant but worked for cruise lines instead. A big smiler, he had a great sense of humor and was a funny story teller who seemed to never forget anyone he ever met or anything he ever did. We joined the Seattle Men's Chorus in 1982 and eventually ended up living in the same big seven-person house on Capitol Hill. Those were the carefree times of disco dancing, one of his great loves. Kevin went to graduate school for a Masters of Social Work. And then his life changed. He struggled with drugs and compulsions and withdrew from those of us around him. It was as if he vanished, sometimes for months on end. Finally, with great determination and the help of Narcotics Anonymous, he came back from the hidden world he had inhabited. He re-emerged sober and apologized to his friends for any hurt he may have caused. To me, he became a closer friend than ever before.

Being disabled with AIDS, Kevin became an active volunteer—with AIDS organizations for many years, with the Washington Statewide Health Insurance Benefits Advisors (SHIBA) assisting needy, confused people obtain health and welfare benefits, and at SeaTac International Airport, just for fun, guiding lost and perplexed travelers to their destinations. He did wear a uniform at the airport, but sadly, it was not a flight attendant's uniform. He would have liked it if it were, especially with color-coordinated heels. Safe travels, my friend.

–Scott Hogan, longtime friend

Table of Contents

Introduction

COMMUNITY MEMBERS OF GenPRIDE, a Seattle-based nonprofit that focuses on the lives of midlife and older LGBTQIA people, authored the stories you are about to read. This dynamic, dedicated group of individuals made a commitment to write their personal experiences in storytelling form to engage and educate the world. The results of their revealing work are in these pages.

As Executive Director of GenPRIDE, I am gratified most by the community-building aspect of this project—which is what GenPRIDE is all about. Community looks different for everyone, especially for LGBTQIA seniors who can find themselves isolated from biological family and living alone. From involvement with this writing workshop, I have learned two key aspects for building community: a common interest and a shared goal. Among these writers, a synergy of communion and solidarity took hold thanks to the connective power of personal storytelling.

These stories will take you directly into the heart and soul of fourteen individuals who worked together for over a year to bring you transformational moments in their lives, sharing some of the deepest secrets they had always held close.

For anyone looking to see what has come from this kind of community-building experience, we invite you to explore the stories that follow.

–Steven Knipp

What participants are saying

- *This was the first writing workshop I have ever participated in because, although I have been writing for my whole life, I always felt intimidated to be in a setting with "real" writers. But, from the start at GenPRIDE and with coach Ingrid Ricks, I felt confident that my voice and personal story would be respected, validated, and nurtured—and my confidence has been amply rewarded. — Irene*

- *It was a very vulnerable experience, but the class was a soft landing pad for this experience. I've taken classes in various settings, but this has to be the most supportive and kind one I've been in, and I was pushed to write much better than I thought I was capable of. — Chris*

- *The class was life-changing for me. I was moved by the honesty of the class members and their courage and levity as they wrote and shared about their lives. It was a great feeling not to be isolated or secretive in my experiences in the Queer community, and to hear how so many acted bravely under tough-ass circumstances. — Nancy*

UNMUTED

The Kids Are All Right

BY IRENE CALVO

THE THREE OF us climb in, Nick whamming the sliding door into lock. Eight years out of Brooklyn and driving a car still feels alien to me, especially today, our planned disaster to the Burke Museum. Did I say disaster? I meant excursion, to the exhibit on the Shackleton polar expedition disaster, which grabbed Nick's attention at school. He is fourteen and Di only eleven, so I still plan family days. Today it's just the three of us, and our destination is more of a decoy, a hope, a wish. The real purpose of our trip is a conversation I dread.

In panic mode, I dash among my galloping thoughts trying to get those horses lined up at the starting gate. I flash on their dad. Suddenly I am in our bedroom. He's been raging at me again, my fault again, he says. Then he recites his favorite refrain at me: "I like the way I am. I don't want to change. If you don't like me, then go find yourself another husband." Little did he know. He smirked gleefully and said it again: "I like the way I am. I don't want to change." He had honed versions of that pithy message for more than two married decades. But he's their dad and they love him, so I've got to keep silent about all that. I return to now. I am here, in the car, with Nick and Di, and I *can* talk about myself. Here we go.

I still seem like normal Mom, even with my insides quivering. My minivan lumbers through the picket-fence neighborhood. Spice Girls start up from the disk. Perfect, no eye contact; that's why I planned this for the car. My throat is parched. Am I really about to come out to my kids? My mind scans possible opening lines like paper globes strung along the silence. All awkward. How much do I disclose, how will they react? Everything I haven't said yet consumes the air in the car. While the kids chatter, in my head ticks a bomb about to detonate their world.

"Ooo, it's Delia calling again," my teenager had taunted just last evening. He doesn't miss anything. How many times had Nick asked me, but I had kept skirting the question: "Mom, are you a lesbian?"

The unruly passion between Delia and me had sprouted like a wild morning glory, as if the seed had long been lodged in my gut. As if the ground were irreparably fertile, and then the rains came. I didn't ask for it and it didn't fit into my world.

It's time now to speak the secret that's been bubbling inside me for months. My cold hands grip the steering wheel hard, eyes grimly focused on the traffic ahead. Nick behind me, Di riding shotgun, I blurt, "Nick has asked me if I am a lesbian." Silence.

"Delia and I are a couple." Silence. "But," I equivocated, "I'm not sure if that makes me a lesbian." What on earth am I saying? Afraid of shattering their world, afraid of disclosing too much, afraid of the fallout to our family life, I am confusing even myself. I turn, see Nick tearful, silent. I had just shoved a big rock and now it was rolling downhill. I felt myself start to fall into exactly the pit I was dreading—sharing this stuff that just felt wrong to be telling them, while it also somehow felt necessary.

Delia and I stole what we called our 'body time' with care, mostly mornings after school drop-off. Our skin bathed by the skylight over her marital bed, time and space collapsed into the vortex of our explorations. My Di and her Ann were schoolmates—as if we needed further complications. Luckily, the girls were too young to notice the scent our bodies must have carried to afternoon school pick-ups.

Our first overnight together waited months until we could zip together a pair of sleeping bags we pinched from Delia's garage. Her husband, Rick, hadn't spied any of my curly hairs shed in their bed but he did notice his sleeping bag went missing. The urgency of our need had made us impervious to both danger and conscience.

When he confronted Delia, "So what *is* your relationship with this woman?" she admitted she had borrowed his bag to zip together with hers on our camping trip. No longer baffled by the vanished sleeping bag, Rick was plain angry. Another thread had been pulled in the unravelling of life as I knew it. Nevertheless, I was stubborn.

"Our relationship won't change anything," I told her. "I won't let it affect my marriage." As if I had any idea.

Unlike her brother, Di remains calm and steady. She doesn't seem to notice any big rock on its way downhill. Nick needles her, annoyed that she doesn't feel as scared as he does about some impending doom without a name.

"Don't you care, Di, about Mom and Delia?" Prompted, she echoes Nick's indignation and upset. Still, she seems oddly determined to make this not matter to her, or at least not to show it right now.

As we drive, we continue to talk about me, and all this. But nothing past the initial impact gets absorbed—yes, Nick's sense was correct. Yes, their mom has something going on with a woman, with the classmate's mom they know. Yes, some doom awaits, though in what form exactly is unknown. It's all true and there is no denying. None of us feels relief, only dread. But for me, the deed has been accomplished.

Outside the Burke, I shift the minivan into park. The three of us turn and look hard at each other, locked in our own minds even while sitting together in this metal box of a family.

"Do you still want to see the Shackleton exhibit?" I venture. Nope, no way. Di is mad at Nick for ruining our excursion. Nick is crying. And I am spent from the words I can't back away from but wish so hard to escape.

We turn around and go home without speaking, my tears falling soundlessly in the silence. Breathe. Drive. Breathe. Somehow, though, even in this terribly unsettled moment, I sense the rightness. I trust Nick and Di to gradually make sense of this conversation and situation, to notice that I stay the same reliable mom. Even without knowing what our future holds, I can tell, the kids will be all right.

IRENE CALVO is a former New Yorker living in Seattle, a pictorial thinker and wordsmith who has had careers as a commercial textile designer, copyeditor, secular homeschooling parent by choice, and litigation paralegal. She is happiest backpacking up mountain trails, sleeping in her tent, and doing pretty much anything with her grown offspring.

The Drive

BY SHAYLA MARIE

THE PLAN WAS to look for the dog. Over the past few weeks, this was becoming a daily event, the dog slipping out the fence, then our frantic search to find him. I turned the truck onto the next block, scanning for a flash of that familiar reddish-brown fur. I glanced over at Travis. His head was smushed against the passenger window, drool dripping from his mouth in a solitary string as the Xanax and heroin took hold. I took the next left.

After several minutes of driving from block to block, I turned out of the residential area onto a different street. A bright green and white freeway exit sign loomed overhead, announcing Highway 18. My thoughts darted erratically, hope opening up beneath anxiety like a bright pink bloom winding its way through concrete, lush and inviting, urgent and insistent. A new plan clawed its way into my mind. *The dog could wait*, I thought. With one hand, I swerved the truck to miss a black sedan, easing onto the freeway on-ramp.

I fumbled over my phone, typing the destination into the GPS. The directions kept loading—before the map flooded the screen in a glorious splash of green and other colors, squiggly twisting lines dancing. Relief flooded my chest. Exactly two hours and twenty-four minutes to Yakima.

∾

LAST NIGHT WAS the final straw for me. Travis shook me from my sleep around two in the morning, roughly yanking my arm, "Where did you put my stuff?!"

"What?" I asked. He was becoming more erratic as the week went on. He hovered over the bed, dressed in all black, his backpack strapped over his shoulders, the funk of the night hanging on him, his body movements jerky, his voice high-pitched.

"My stuff!"

"What stuff?"

"I gave it to you!" He screamed, smashing an open palm against the nearby wall. He tore his backpack off, slamming it on the bed, ripping it open to rummage through the pockets. "Where is it?"

"I don't have your stuff," I whispered, fear curling around my shoulders. As the drugs took over, they smothered his inhibitions, increasing his angry outbursts, his intense physical reactions, anger overflowing like red lava.

"Fuck! Fuck! Fuck!" Travis raced across the room to the dresser, yanking drawers loose with a screech, leaving them to hang open like gaping mouths as he searched. I sat up in the bed. He turned away from me, pulling a piece of smoke-stained foil from his pocket. He laid it on the dresser, a small plastic tube clutched in his hand. I rolled over in the bed, turning my back to him, hearing the scratchy flick of a lighter. I pulled the comforter over my head, burrowing in the warmth and safety of the blankets, dread filling my body. *I couldn't wait until Friday.*

Travis was set to go to rehab on Friday, a place in Yakima called Sunshine Ranch. This would be his first long-time stint at rehab after numerous outpatient programs and failed counseling attempts, broken promises to change made and discarded like litter amongst his burnt pieces of foil and tiny smudged baggies. As the rehab countdown began, his normal drug use grew to a non-stop frenzy, days and nights of mixing multiple substances like Xanax, meth, heroin, and marijuana into a toxic cocktail, substances lit with that hot blue flame on a tiny piece of scorched foil, melting them into unconscious nights, nights spent passed out curled up in a ball, sweaty and pale, his breathing shallow and erratic. It was only Tuesday. *He's not going to make it*, I thought.

I awoke to find him passed out on the living room floor. My blood pressure surged. *Not again*, I thought, squatting next to him. He was clammy, his skin sallow, a thin sweat covering his forehead. His white T-shirt stuck to his skin, stained dark with black heroin smudges, his jeans pulled half off. After several shakes, his eyes opened to tiny razor-thin slits, drool slipping out the corner of his chapped lips. He turned his head to glare at me.

I can't keep doing this if he doesn't go. If he doesn't leave for rehab, then I will leave, I thought. I struggled to help him up onto the couch. It had been years of this. Years of lies; months of broken promises; days of manipulation; hours, minutes and seconds all squandered on him, feeding his addiction and trying to "save" him. There had to be a point where I saved myself. I had to free myself from this addiction, even if he didn't.

If you've never closely known anyone dealing with addiction, being the sober girlfriend of an addict is like living on a deserted island of Alone, an island with dull gray waves and jagged gray rocks, a stone gray sky, and an ashen tide for miles with only your isolation and depressed thoughts to keep you company. When your loved one is sober, you see the bloom of a bright orange raft in the distance, the firework flash of a flare in that gray sky; then the next day, you come home to see that life raft submerged, him in a heroin haze, half awake, weaving around like a zombie. I would coax him to bed, pulling off stained jeans and tugging off too-tight shoes. After pulling a blanket over him, I often laid next to him listening for his breath, watching his chest rise and fall.

Things hadn't always been this way between us. Our life used to be whispered promises under a cocoon of blankets in the middle of the night, the warmth of our mingled breath as he came close, his head tipped against mine, the heat of his skin as he wrapped me in, before his casual love of pills became a rampant love affair with heroin. In the beginning, it was nights on the couch, watching reruns of whatever sitcom was on, him twisting my hair between his fingers, feeding me popcorn kernel by kernel between kisses, soft and slow. But now nights were spent with me sitting, watching, and waiting for the other shoe to drop, waiting for the night he didn't wake up, waiting for him to come home from one of his dealers' homes, or waiting for him to come out of the bathroom, where he'd been smoking whatever substance was handy, a cloud of fragrant metallic smoke surrounding him like a fog when he opened the door, stumbling out, eyes glazed, skin bright pink. Those old moments kept me strong, kept me focused, kept me trapped. I hoped for those old moments. Thoughts of the "old" Travis kept my love alive. I held those old memories to my chest, another life raft.

✦

ANOTHER HOUR TO Yakima. The miles passed fast, chasing one another recklessly. My foot pressed the gas in desperation. Snippets of scenery flashed by, freeway signs in green and white, flashes of scarlet brake lights, cars whizzing past, and mileage markers counting down the miles. From time to time Travis rustled, causing my breath to catch; after a moment his cheek fell back to caress his glass pillow. After he settled, I gunned the gas, the speedometer creeping past one hundred.

A bright amber light popped up on the dash, catching my eye. The gas was on E, the pointer firmly pressing the line. This was the problem with plans changing. We were in the middle of nowhere. Just miles of asphalt gray, lumbering trees and the encroaching night surrounding us, dusk melting the sky into burnished pink decorated with dashes of gray velvet. *We can make it*, I thought, pressing on the gas. *Fuck*.

"Where are we?" Travis asked. I jumped in surprise, turning to see him fully awake, looking around, studying the scenery, his features tight with anger. "Where are we, Shayla?"

"We're going to Sunshine Ranch."

"What!" He bashed his fist against the passenger window, "Go back now!"

I drove on, tears blooming fresh, running down my cheeks. My foot crushed the speedometer until it hurt.

"Fuck this," he said, searching through his pockets, the seat, the console, the deep pockets on the door. "Where's my phone?" He snatched my phone from the cup holder, clearing out the map in a zap, tapping the emergency call button. "Yes, hello!" he said, "I'm being kidnapped!"

The gas light glowed brighter, taunting me as I pressed hard on the gas. *Cmon*, I thought, *just fifty more minutes.*

"We're on the freeway in a black Chevy truck. A 2000, I think." His voice frustrated, "No, I don't know where!"

I'm not going back, I thought, not going back to the knocked-out nights, the confused conversations, the drugged dawns, watching on guard as he slept, waiting for his chest to fall, my cheek pressed against his lips to feel the heat of his breath. *I can't do it,* I thought, *I can't live like this anymore.* And, he wouldn't live like this much longer.

"I'm supposed to go to treatment on Friday," he whispered. "I promised my dad."

I felt numb, tears colliding with the landscape of my face, thoughts and negative memories running over me, snippets of his conversation bursting through at odd moments.

"No, she's not stopping. We're almost to exit 68." He shoved the phone towards me. "Here."

"Hello Shayla, this is Candy, I'm a 911 dispatcher," a soft voice coaxed.

"Okay." I heard distant sirens tearing through the silence of the night.

"The state patrol is going to need you to pull over. They need more information about what's going on."

I smashed the power button on the phone until the front screen collapsed, along with my hopes. This was addiction—a complete lack of hope, a complete loss of control, a complete destruction of faith. Addiction was a runaway freight train tearing a path through your life and the people who loved you, along with this feeling, this helpless, listless, dead-inside feeling where nothing would ever get better. I wore this feeling like a second skin.

I fooled myself into believing that I could control this, make him better, save him. But I couldn't save him. I couldn't even save myself. I couldn't control anything about this situation. *What was I thinking? He was not ready for this,* I thought. Someone else's addiction can't be controlled. If this addiction was going to be captured, Travis needed to cast the net. I drove on, my thoughts racing with desperation.

What would the police say? I didn't know.

Would they understand how much he needed to go to rehab? Probably not.

Could they arrest me? Maybe!

I need to save myself. All I can control is my own life.

The exit sign came. The exit sign went. I drove past exit 68. I glanced in the rearview mirror, red and blue lights blooming up in the distance like fireworks, the hypnotic blare of the sirens flooding the cab of the truck. I kept driving as the flashing lights and piercing sirens receded, turning down the sloped ramp of the exit.

"What in the fuck are you doing?" Travis demanded, his voice rising with each slam of his hand against the dash. "Pull … Over … Now!"

I saw a highway sign announcing "Gas Next Right." The gas station sat directly off the exit. I coasted to an empty pump. I sat defeated, tears streaking my cheeks, hands gripping the steering wheel, staring ahead, that familiar numb feeling smothering me like smog.

I tried.

I failed.

There was nothing else I could do.

Addiction won.

Again.

Sitting there, the pain of the past four years of this, this fight, this push and pull with him and the drugs weighed on me. He always chose the drugs. I needed to choose differently for myself. I wasn't going to do this anymore. Once we got home, I would start packing my things. Addiction wasn't going to beat me down or steal another hour, minute, or second of my life. If he decided to change, I would be there. If not, I was going to save myself. I would put myself first for once.

"Where are we going now?" He asked impatiently, patting his

pockets, searching for his cigarette pack.

I took a deep breath, studying his face, "We're going home."

SHAYLA MARIE was born and raised in Seattle, a place that cultivated her love of reading, writing, and the arts since childhood. Now a single mother of three teenaged children, she is focused on spreading the love of writing and creativity through creativity coaching and creativity groups. Check out her website for more information, www.shaylamariewrites.com.

Journey's End ... a Beginning

BY JENNY ROBINSON

I SQUINTED IN THE bright July sun as I walked along the platform toward my car and caught the reflection of a confident and proud woman in the windows and on the sides of the shiny rail cars. A woman on her way to her destiny, a destiny incubating in her soul for sixty-nine years. My consciousness was flooded with one thought, "I'm doing it, I am actually doing it!"

Finding my seat and settling in, my mind flooded with thoughts and memories. As the train lurched forward with its ever-present clackity-clack, I was thinking about the question that so many had been asking me recently, "Are you excited?" Well, of course I was, but not in the overwhelming sense that I had anticipated. With a smile, I allowed myself to be bathed in peace, a peace that I had sought desperately for many years.

Looking out the windows at the scenery rushing by, I allowed my thoughts to wander back to that night very long ago.

It was New Year's Eve. I was barely three years old. My older brother and I had just awakened from our naps and were playing in Mom and Dad's bedroom. I was terribly excited that I was going to be able to stay up and share in this grown-up celebration. Mom must have just done a laundry before the family arrived, and the pile was on their bed waiting to be folded. I noticed a pretty pair of panties and went over to touch them. I remembered how nice they always felt to touch. Then, without much thought, I picked them up, stepped into the leg openings, and pulled them up, just as I think most little girls might do, right over my pajamas. Mom happened to walk in right then and, thinking that it was very cute, she scooped me up and carried me downstairs to show everyone. There was some laughter, which was certainly not malicious, and some ooooos and giggles from the women. It wasn't embarrassing, but I somehow also realized that it was cute because the little boy I was supposed to be shouldn't have put them on.

I was stirred out of my reveries by the "Tickets, please!" of the conductor. As he handed my ticket back with a "Thank you, have a nice trip Ma'am," I smiled back with a "I suspect I will."

Looking at the bright sun through the tinted glass made me think of sitting on those hard carpeted stairs in our hallway when I was eight years old. I sat there with the morning edition of the Baltimore Sun, reading and rereading the front page story. My mind was racing. It was really possible! It was right there! This beautiful woman on the front page of the paper, whose name was

Christine Jorgensen, had just come back from Denmark where she had had what was then known as a sex-change surgery. My eight-year-old mind yelled back, Sure it's possible, but it probably costs more than a million dollars but, ever being a bit stubborn, again I whispered to myself, "But, oh my ... it's really possible!"

That tattered piece of newsprint never did fall completely apart; well, not without the help of a great deal of scotch tape. It was safely hidden away in my secret space between the floor joists in the attic, in my tiny stash of "me things." I don't remember very much of what was there, other than a pair of panties that I had somehow managed to screw up enough courage to buy at the five-and-dime store with my saved-up allowance.

Sigh! My tiny stash of "me things!" So very much hiding! So very much frustration! So much hatred for that male appendage and its accompanying testosterone poisoning, ruining my body. I didn't want a beard! I didn't want a deep voice! I wanted soft breasts growing on my chest.

How does one describe something that is so completely intangible, yet at the same time so tangible that it holds your soul in its grip, a grip so tight that one cannot move away from or loosen it. The internal angst cinches a little more tightly each time we accede to and conform more to what the world calls for our image to be.

I thought about the time I tried to somehow explain the feelings to my wife. I told her it was as if something were always just out of kilter. No matter how small or insignificant it was, nothing felt quite right. She scoffed at that, as most cis people do. It is impossible to imagine what living in the wrong body is like.

As they usually did, my thoughts along this line wandered back to what was a turning point of my marriage. Serving as a eucharistic minister at our church was very special, and I loved doing it.

One night my wife came downstairs where I was doing some studying, and asked, "When you serve, do you wear women's underthings?"

"Uh, yes, of course," I said, looking up from my book.

"Well, don't you think that is offensive to God?"

As I sat looking up at her, my mind was like a pinball that had just been released and was bouncing all over the place, wondering where this had come from and what had precipitated it. Perhaps worse was about where it was going. I replied, "No, I feel that I am being respectful. I am serving as myself."

With a noncommittal, "Oh," she turned and went back upstairs, leaving me with lingering thoughts and doubts as to potential scenarios and how they might play out, none of which ended happily.

Hiding! Oh, I so hated hiding! Hiding things! Hiding self! Hiding life! In the past nearly-four years since the marriage had fallen apart, I had been able to let go of a great deal of it. This trip down to Portland was going to eliminate a lot more.

I had become so adept at playing my different roles as a way of maneuvering through life, I rarely got caught. Then again, it only took one time to realize that I had jeopardized my whole future for a few minutes of feeling free ... of feeling alive.

It must have been around 2:00 in the morning. I had just

returned to the campus and parked my car after a short walk downtown dressed as a woman. I was walking back to the dorm when I became aware that a campus patrol car had noticed and had begun following me. Finally cornering me, the security officer got out and walked toward me, blinding me with his large flashlight.

"Get in!" Panic seized me as he pointed towards the car and again ordered, "Get in!"

My mind was racing like a cornered animal, eyes darting everywhere, seeking someplace to run and hide. Grasping for some nonexistent sanctuary, I saw my whole future evaporating as he pointed to the patrol car.

"What is your name? Are you a student here at Ithaca?"

I numbly nodded my head, muttering my name and dorm number, hoping that would make this nightmare end.

"What is your major?"

"Theatre, sir."

"What are you doing out in the parking lot at this time of the night?"

I grasped for anything at all that could even remotely be considered a reasonable explanation for why I was in a dress and wearing makeup.

"Oh! I just got finished with a rehearsal down at the theatre, and they wanted to lock up," I lied.

"Is there anyone who can vouch for you?"

Sure, I could think of a dozen right off the top of my head. But! But, whomever I chose was also going to be made aware of my deeply hidden secret.

"Well, can you think of anybody?"

"Oh, sorry, Officer, I was trying to think of someone who might still be up at this time of the night and not be disturbed. Say, you know who Marty Nadler is, don't you? You can call Marty."

Everybody on campus knew who Marty was. He was the funny man on campus. Ever a quick wit and one of the funniest people I've ever known, he always looked as though he were on his way to do a show in the Catskills. Well, it seemed that I had chosen well.

Pointing to the squad car, "Get in the back there, and we'll go to the office and call him."

I sat there in the harsh fluorescent light of the campus police office, waiting and praying, "Oh, please be there, Marty!" Other than a pretty trench coat because of the weather, I have no idea what I was wearing. My only memory was of sheer mortification, coupled with fear ... and just waiting.

"Okay, you're good to go. Marty spoke very highly of you. Oh, and uh, try to find some way to change before leaving the theatre next time."

I had made the right choice! Marty's and my paths continued to cross on campus, but nothing was ever said. Pretty remarkable for 1967 or '68.

Now, as the train crossed over the Columbia River, I kept saying to myself, "My goodness, girl, you're really going to pull this off. You know, you have a right to feel proud." I thought of a lifetime of prayers, a lifetime of hopes and dreams, a lifetime of wishes, yet never daring to believe that they could be fulfilled. I remembered when Kaiser announced that it would cover GCS, Gender Confirmation Surgery. The medical profession had come to the conclusion, finally, that the only way to reconcile the dysphoria that plagues those of us who are transgender was to make the body match the mind and create a single whole person.

It had been just about ten years since I had taken that first little white estrogen tablet. Ten years filled with so much loss … my company, my marriage, my home, my family, and most everything else of meaning in my life. What I had found through all of that loss, though, was peace, an inner peace that had eluded me for sixty-nine years. I was no longer in conflict with myself to merely survive. I was becoming a whole woman, with all of the strength and pride that comes with it. Sixty-nine years of hidden pain and frustration to be let go and become only a fading memory. That little girl had finally grown up.

I had lost nearly everything, but I had found peace … I had found myself!

JENNY ROBINSON has a degree in theatre and her chosen fine art form is traditional Chinese brushstroke painting. She has written for most of her life and has always been fascinated by word play. Her three-act play has been produced while her complex fantasy novel is still living on her tablet. She has also composed numerous theological talks and essays.

A Journey Without You

BY STEVEN KNIPP

I WOKE UP STARTLED and wasn't sure why. Had I been dreaming? It was silent—devoid of the hacking cough that rattled my bedroom walls most mornings. I headed to the spare room to check on Tom. But as I neared the door, my eyes caught on his overstuffed chair in the living room. It had been clocked 180 degrees and was now facing the wall. As my mind began to register this, I noticed that Tom was in it. All I could see was the top of his head and his left arm dangling over the armrest, both unmoving. At first I couldn't process the scene, but when my eyes took in two envelopes taped to the back of the chair, I froze. Our conversations about his suicide planning came flooding back—the why, the how, and the fact that I'd be with him when he died. What had he done? I ran toward him, thinking it might not be too late to save him, but when I touched his stone-cold arm, I knew he was gone. I looked reluctantly at his face—it was frozen, lifeless, pale blue. On the floor was an empty bottle of pills. A white flash of pain suddenly blinded me. I collapsed at his feet, sobbing uncontrollably.

As I laid there trying to catch my breath, my mind returned to the day Tom first brought up suicide. It was after his second prolonged hospital stay when he broached the subject. We were standing in the kitchen putting away groceries and Tom was winded from the mild exertion. Being reminded of his physical weakness after minor activity always exasperated him.

"What's the point?" he said defeatedly. "My life is going to end anyway, so why should I be fighting so hard?" Over the past year Tom had spent countless hopeful hours reading and talking to experts about curing himself of AIDS, but now he looked completely dejected. "I'm so sick of being sick," he went on. He looked away for a moment, then returned his gaze to mine. "I need to tell you about something I've been holding back for months." This sounded serious. I looked at him intently and nodded for him to continue.

"The last hospital visit scared me. I felt trapped like a prisoner. I don't want to die hooked up to tubes in a hospital, languishing day after day doped up on morphine, half out of it, until I die. I don't want to go like that." It hurt to hear the pain in his voice, and I wasn't sure where he was going with this. Seeing the confusion on my face, he reached over and took my hand before continuing, "I've lost control of everything. It was something I prided myself in, that ability to control my destiny. I had a plan. As soon as we met, I started pinching pennies to save for a down payment on a house. We moved here together to make a life, but now that's over." Anxiety washed over me as I braced myself for what was next. "I want to take control of the way I die," he stated matter-of-factly, pausing a moment before continuing. "I've been making a plan to commit suicide when the time is right."

A switch flipped in my brain, shutting down my comprehension of his words. Did he just say he wanted to kill himself? I could feel my shoulders hunch up as I folded my arms around myself. "You want to commit suicide?" I heard myself asking quietly. We had been through so much to keep him hopeful, and now he just wanted to give up? A cocktail of sadness and anger surged through me as I tried to keep myself from running out of the room.

"Not right now, no," he assured me. "I want to have a plan though, to figure out the details of how best to do it. I'll relax if I have something figured out." My brain could understand what he was saying, but my heart felt like it was being shoved through a meatgrinder.

"What kind of plan do you mean?" I managed.

"How I'm going to kill myself," he replied. Before I had a chance to react to that bombshell, he moved on to explaining. "It's more difficult than you think." He was suddenly animated, his eyes bright with excitement. "Especially if you don't want to leave a mess, which rules out guns, wrist cutting, or jumping off a building. The options you're left with are carbon monoxide poisoning or drugs. I figure that pills are the best option…" and then he stopped talking, noticing my mouth had dropped open. The words guns, carbon monoxide, and leaving a mess were bouncing around in my head. Were we really having this conversation? He made it sound like he was talking about which ice cream flavor to choose. Had I been so distracted with school that I had no clue what he had been consumed with? "Sorry about that," he finally said. "I've been thinking about this for months, alone, so I got comfortable with the subject. I didn't mean to overwhelm you." He gave my hand a squeeze, then asked what I was thinking.

What was I thinking? For starters, how about *Why the hell have you been planning to leave me?* But that quickly became overshadowed by another terrifying thought—what if he does this without me knowing? I tucked away my feelings and forced myself to sound supportive and understanding.

"Well, let me see. You're right about our comfort levels with the topic—I'm not there yet." I paused as my lip trembled and I fought back the urge to cry. Tom pulled me closer and remained silent. I went on. "I don't want you to die in a hospital either, so you should have a plan and get whatever drugs you need." I sat back so I could look at him. "I'm also clear about this," I stressed, locking my eyes on his. "I want to be with you when you die. I don't want to be surprised by finding your body one day." These were hard words to say because I had no idea what I was getting myself into. I concentrated on appearing interested in his plans as my insides were full of turmoil, wondering if I could really do this.

In the months that followed, planning his death was all Tom talked about. It became surprisingly easy to discuss it with him. I reacted supportively to everything he said but I also refused to accept the prospect of it actually happening. That all changed after having lunch with our friend Paul, who told us about a suicide party he recently attended.

"Suicide party?" I asked. I had never heard of such a thing. My stomach flinched at the sound of it. How could anything be more ghoulish than referring to suicide as a party?

"Oh, it's the latest thing guys with AIDS are doing," he replied. "A friend of mine had a fabulous vacation on the credit card he knew he'd never have to repay, then he planned an elaborate send-off party with his friends." I looked over at Tom, who was transfixed. Paul went on describing the scene. "When I showed up, the house was filled with people and music and booze. Lots of conversation and laughing while the soon-to-be-dead regaled his closest friends with stories of his life. When the appointed time came, he gathered everyone around for the moment that would start his self-deliverance." By now, I was imagining Tom swallowing pills as I watched. Would I be strong enough to sit by and watch him kill himself? What would I do when he stopped breathing? Would I freak out and try to resuscitate him? It's one thing to imagine being brave to support him, but would be quite another to see it actually happen.

Paul continued, "The entire room turned their full attention to him; he said how glad he was that we were all there. Then he told us about his biggest fear: dying alone. Through stifled sobs he said that wasn't going to happen now. It was all very moving."

And that's when the logic of Tom's decision finally made sense to me. He didn't want to be alone—of course! This way he could surround himself with loved ones instead of dying in a cold hospital setting. It stopped seeming like such a selfish thing to do. I felt lighter for the first time since this whole talk of suicide began. Plus, I couldn't argue with his happier disposition since he had stockpiled a lethal dose of pills.

Once we left Paul's house, Tom knew just what he wanted to do. "I know my sister will come, and probably my mom and dad," he said during the car ride home. I sat in the passenger seat wishing we could talk about anything else. I did my best to be encouraging, but I couldn't shut out the cacophony of voices that were screaming in my mind. I knew everything he was planning was about to come true.

❧

I DON'T KNOW how much time I spent at the foot of Tom's lifeless body before I remembered the letters. I jumped up and looked at the envelopes taped to the chair back. I pulled off the envelope with my name on it and quickly opened it, desperate to hear his voice even if it was written on a page. His familiar scrawl brought on a new round of grief as I read his words through tear-filled eyes.

I'm so scared! A journey without you, it will be so lonely! I choose to commit suicide without your knowledge and do hope you will not consider this a breach of our trust. My reasons for doing things this way was to spare you any guilt you might feel for not stopping me, and also to prevent any questions from the authorities as to why you didn't stop me. I love you more than you could ever imagine. You have enhanced the quality of my life a million times and I do hope we will meet in the future so we can continue our beautiful relationship. Until then, grieve quickly and let life go on. Love, Tom.

I let out a cry of anguish, his last words tearing me in two.

Looking back at the start of the letter, my eyes focused on his opening words—he was scared. He had no idea what to expect once he swallowed the pills and he must have been terrified. The vision of him sitting all alone, waiting to die, broke my heart. But as I kept reading, my grief turned to betrayal. He hoped I wouldn't think this a breach of trust? How could it be anything but that? He lied to me. We had an agreement and he broke his promise that I could be there with him at the end. I didn't even get to say goodbye. The months of planning and talking and preparation was all for nothing. I tossed the note on the floor and began reading the second one marked for the authorities.

To whom it may concern: I have decided to end my life because the suffering of my disease is unbearable to me. This decision is known to others but the final decision has been mine alone in a normal state of mind. I am a member of the Hemlock Society ....

I stopped mid-sentence. I had forgotten all about his membership at Hemlock, an organization that supports the right to die. I picked up the phone and dialed Tom's caseworker who had told me to call if anything happened. When Randy answered the phone, my voice cracked.

"He did it ... he's gone." We had talked about Tom so there was no need to say more. He knew exactly how to respond.

"I'll call the coroner," he said after expressing his condolences. "Are you still with him?"

"Yes," I managed, looking over at Tom's corpse. I stared at the lifeless body, my head spinning, unable to reconcile the surrealness of it.

"Are you okay?" Randy asked after a few moments of silence.

I was expecting this question because he had told us that the risk was high I might try to kill myself.

"I'm as okay as you might expect, but I'm not suicidal," I replied to put his mind at ease. The last thing I wanted was for him to come racing over with a shrink in tow. "Seriously, I'm fine." After hanging up, I went into the kitchen to get away from the body. As the minutes ticked away waiting for the coroner, my mind flashed to the day before. The AIDS quilt was in town and we decided to attend. The quilt stretched for hundreds of yards, comprised of thousands of unique three-by six-foot panels devoted to individuals who had died. Each quilted panel displayed a collage of a life: photographs, writings, artworks, and fabrics of all kinds. It was impossible not to think about a good friend of ours who had died just a few days earlier. Tom was close to him. As we slowly walked the convention center pathways with hundreds of others, the silence in the enormous room was deafening. The sole exception was a woman's soft voice coming from the stage slowly reading names—"Michael Adams," she read from the page in front of her, followed by a long pause where stillness rushed in. Then she called out the next one, "Stephanie Milton," followed by another long gap of silence. Her voice became the metronome of death, of lives lost too soon. We walked up and down the pathways, our predicament coming back into full view. We both had AIDS. Tom was already sick. My blood tests were dismal. All I could think about was my name on one of those quilts.

At home that evening, Tom was surprisingly affectionate and insisted we bathe together. He had dropped his usual reserve about me witnessing his emaciated body. We soaped one another and touched with tenderness. As we towel dried each other slowly, I felt intimate with him for the first time in years. There were no words, just the warmth of his touch and an intense rush of fondness. Afterward, we settled on the couch to watch "Married with Children," our nightly routine. Emotionally and physically drained, I drifted to sleep in front of the TV. Tom woke me and walked me to the bedroom. I crawled under the covers groggy with sleep. He perched on the edge of the bed and looked at me intently; then leaned over and kissed my forehead.

"You know how much I love you, don't you?" he asked. I smiled and nodded yes and gave him a hug goodnight. He continued to look at me, wordless. Something in the way he was watching—with clear eyes and a peaceful expression—gave me pause, a sense I disregarded. Tom turned off the light and left.

❧

THERE WAS NO way to deny the brutal reality of what had happened as I watched Tom's corpse be placed into a black bag, zipped up, and taken out of the house on a gurney. When the door closed I dropped to the couch. My body felt heavy and defeated. Nothing remained but a chilling silence. Tom was gone and I would never see him again. My thoughts flew back to the previous night and how the AIDS quilt must have solidified his decision—how could I have missed that? Why hadn't I been more attentive as he told me how much he loved me? Why hadn't I told him I loved him back? I should have pulled him next to me in the bed and held him tight. A fresh wave of grief washed over me, my body trembling as I replayed our last moments together.

It was the last time he would touch me, the last time he would say he loved me. My mind fixated on what the note had said. *My reasons for doing things this way was to spare you any guilt you might feel for not stopping me.* What wasn't in that sentence was the excruciating subtext. He wasn't trying to spare my guilt; he was afraid I would intervene. It had been one of the things we spoke about because once he fell asleep he would no longer be in control; he knew there was a possibility I might call 911. I had assured him I wouldn't, but he wasn't willing to take that chance. He chose not to trust me. And while that stung, I also knew he was right—I would have tried to save him. As the weight of this truth pinned me down, my body shook with heartache. Tom was everything to me; he was my first love and the man I trusted with my life. Now he was gone and I was next.

An agonizing pressure started in the pit of my stomach and barreled past my lips as I screamed out an unexpressed misery that was now clear and present. I was not safe from the same fate as Tom. I collapsed to the floor in a crumpled ball, sobbing inconsolably as the reality of my situation hit: I was only twenty-nine years old and it was just a matter of time before the body in the black bag would be mine.

 **STEVEN KNIPP** is the Executive Director of GenPRIDE. The story in this anthology is the opening chapter of his soon-to-be-published memoir: *Fearfully, Wonderfully Made.* He has been in Seattle for 30 years, and currently lives in the Columbia City neighborhood with his family.

Blood Sisters

BY AMY D. RUBIN

IN LOVING MEMORY of Susan Blalock, 1957-2020

Ladybird, ladybird fly away home,
Your house is on fire,
Your children shall burn!

From *Tommy Thumb's Pretty Song Book*, England, 1744

Prologue
February 10, 2011—Lake Forest Park, Washington

IT ALL STARTED with a fire. It began in Mom's bedroom when the electric heater shorted out and burst into flames just inches away from her bed and her ninety-four-year-old head of fine white hair. She awoke with a start, sat up, and with the help of her walker dragged herself to the top of the stairs that led down to my studio. Then she began to scream out my name.

I was downstairs practicing Debussy at the piano, oblivious to the rest of the world, lost in musical reverie. Mom was certain I would die if her calls did not reach me, but she was not one to panic. Finally I heard her voice, hoarse from shouting above the music. As I raced upstairs, a series of bomb-like explosions circled me as one by one windows shattered and fragments of glass flew through the air. I was dazed, paralyzed, transfixed by this grotesque spectacle as seen from the perspective of a front row seat. I watched the beige curtains shrivel and turn first orange and then black as flames engulfed and swallowed them.

Mom snapped, "We have to get out now," awakening me from my trance. I grabbed my phone in one hand and with the other took her arm. "Hurry," she said. Together we escaped into a downpour. Mom closed the front door firmly behind her to contain the fire. She didn't have time to find her shoes so with only thin socks to protect her fragile feet she followed me up our muddy hill to safety.

A few weeks later, I began to experience intense jolts that felt like electric shocks, first in my fingers, then arms, then torso. Drying my back with a towel felt like someone cutting into my skin with an electric saw. I heard myself whimper. Not only was the searing pain horrific, my worry about what was causing it was even worse. I was certain I would soon die, as only something serious could cause these symptoms, which initially were sporadic but now attacked me all the time. My anxiety was barely manageable as I thought, *This is what a nervous breakdown must feel like.* Still, I did my best to be the caretaker of our household, working long days with teams of movers, inspectors, and firemen to clear the ash and fumes that were left behind. Ninety-five percent of everything Mom owned had burned. I had to buy her underwear, tops, bottoms, nightgowns, robes, jackets, shoes, gloves, and cosmetics. And our insurance policy required that we estimate a price for each item destroyed before we were permitted to replace it.

"Mom, I'm going shopping. Tell me what you need the most."

"Curlers," she mumbled.

Mom wept during our meeting with the adjuster. "How can I put a value on Amy's baby shoes?" I didn't even know she had saved them for fifty-nine years with her valuables. I had always thought of Mom as strong and stoical but now as I watched her unravel, I found myself feeling powerless and angry, especially when she said she was ready for her life to end.

In the months that followed, both my mother and I would be diagnosed with cancer, hers breast, mine blood. Looking back, I would feel like there was the time before and then the time after the fire. The fireman had extinguished the initial raging blaze in a matter of minutes, but my memories and fears from that day would smolder like embers for years to come.

Blood 1
February 11, 2011—Comfort Inn, Aurora Avenue. Seattle, Washington

THE ROOM IS stuffy and the walls thin. The TV next door transmits a low murmur. Periodically a laugh track erupts. I am tempted to knock softly on the wall in protest, but am distracted by a strange burning that has begun in my fingertips. Something somewhere is wrong.

Too many platelets may cause blood clots or strokes in those with counts over 1,000,000 or in those over the age of 60 with elevated counts. ET (essential thrombocytosis) is the name of this rare condition that in approximately 3% of cases will convert into a leukemia that is quick moving and frequently fatal. Related cancers, such as PV (polycythemia vera) and MF (myelofibrosis) are MPNs (myeloproliferative disorders), which affect white blood cells, red blood cells and platelets. In most cases, genetic mutations such as the Jak 2 are determined to be the cause.

The steering wheel is searing hot and its heat seems to flow into the palms of my hands, especially along the lifelines. I wonder if the chill of a cold soda can might cool the sensations enough so that I can continue the long drive to the Peninsula. But I can barely grasp the can. Just the contact of it against my fingertips is excruciating.

Standard recommended medications for MPNs include HU (Hydroxyurea) as the first drug of choice. Possible side effects may include leg ulcers, hair loss, violent headaches, and nausea. Some scientists believe that taking HU may cause ET to convert to leukemia over time. Still, it remains the first line drug of choice for treatment.

Sensations like shooting stars begin across my torso. Red dots decorate my thighs which were once a pure and an uncompromised white. My body has been taken over by some mysterious force; my body has become a strange canvas. Who is the painter?

Blood 2

May 24, 2011—Swedish Hospital. Seattle, Washington (as if in a dream)

THEY SEND YOU back to Dr. X to confirm the details of your blood draw. Should they check for the Jak 2 mutation again? The nurses and support staff occupy different workstations.  Back here is their private world where they joke about too much garlic in the phở they brought in for lunch.

Dr. X moves easily among them, responding with signatures, explanations, and referrals. The phone rings constantly as he slips in and out of his office managing a seemingly endless flow of details and demands. You notice the photographs of wildlife that cover most of the back room wall. One closeup is of a grizzly, most likely from Alaska, holding a giant salmon between a set of large gleaming teeth. This hospital art is an interesting partner to the large tank of tropical fish in the waiting room. *What is this fish theme all about?* you wonder.

Then you see the elegant lady you had noticed when you checked in—the one who had been sitting right next to the tropical fish. She can't be sick. She is too pretty and her mauve handbag matches her perfectly tailored and one-of-a-kind mauve scarf and pantsuit, all too elegant for a waiting room, all too festive for a visit to an oncologist.

But now she is back here with the medical staff huddled, almost squeezed, into a vacant corner with Dr. X. You hear her voice, which is as smooth as her wardrobe, nothing out of place, but her words are not what you should be hearing. You did not choose to be standing here as their witness.

"I'll travel anywhere for any drug. Please. There must be something else I can try." She says this with a tone devoid of emotion. You wonder what prep school she attended, probably one of the best on the East Coast where they teach you never to show weakness and to always appear perfectly groomed and grammatically correct even when you are dying.

She tries again a number of times with different words filling in for those she first spoke. You wonder which cost more, her scarf or her handbag or a dose of medication? Dr. X shakes his head emphatically, and you hear him say, "No. There is nothing, nothing more we can do."

They stand just a few feet away from you but they appear not to notice you and because of this you are forced into a kind of hospital voyeurism. You hope he'll get to the part where he says he is sorry, or maybe he spoke too quickly and in fact there is somewhere she can travel to get that pill that might add at least some days on to her life while they look for other pills, but that part of the conversation never comes. You hope he will at least give her a hug, but no; instead he turns away. He has many other patients who are waiting for him and at least there is a chance that *they* can be helped. Your heart is beating fast. Your heart is breaking.

This could be you.

Blood 3

Jan 2013—Westlake Avenue. Seattle, Washington

THE PARKING LOT in back the of Azteca restaurant has very few cars and is littered with cigarette butts, empty bottles of cheap gin, and a few condoms. It's 11 a.m. and really too early for lunch.

I've driven down to Westlake in the grey drizzle for the meeting of the Seattle Myeloproliferative Neoplasms (MPNs) Cancer Support group. I was diagnosed with ET close to two years ago and hope to find others who might become a source of support and comfort. This is my second time attending and truthfully, I would rather be drinking the preparation for a colonoscopy. Whose brilliant idea was it to mix a discussion about doctors, drugs, and deaths with pungent smells of tacos, a garish decor of saints and skeletons screaming with bright colors, and a soundtrack of syrupy mariachi music?

An old silver Toyota pulls in slowly on the other side of the parking lot. A woman with long greying hair turns off the ignition and sits as if waiting for something. I'm pretty sure she has come for the meeting, and like me is hoping that someone or something will give her an alternative to going inside. I have the instant feeling of liking her, which is strange given how much I am not liking anything or anyone these days.

In my mind, I review the cast of characters I will be seeing again. Jane has ET like me, and joined CrossFit to get pumped and super healthy. She hardly opens her mouth other than to eat surprisingly large portions of protein. Her husband, Fred, sits next to her and answers all the questions that come her way so she can chew without distraction. Paul is red-faced, either from the elevated red cells of PV or his anger about the *motherfucking doctors* who aren't doing their jobs of controlling his hematocrit. I wonder if the disease has made him explosive or if he was born this way.

Two people, Jake and Marge, have MF, the disease where you're not dead yet but you're potentially on your way to leukemia. She's thin and he in turn is bulky. They both are contemplating the excruciatingly frightening future of a bone marrow transplant to keep them alive, and given their conditions, each looks surprisingly strong.

Back in the parking lot, the lady with the greying hair and I cautiously exit our vehicles and sneak into the ladies room, hoping that no one in the group has spotted us. We wash our hands in adjacent sinks as our eyes connect in the mirrors.

"Are you here for the support meeting?"

"Yup," she answers and we sigh in synchronicity. "I literally forced myself to come," she continues.

"Me too. Hey, want to catch a movie instead?" I ask. We laugh, and in that moment I sense that I may have found an ally. I sure could use one.

Blood 4

February 2013 – August 2017—Seattle and Hansville, Washington and other places

My new friend is Susan, Sooze for short. We are Mutt and Jeff, her larger-boned, tall frame compared to my elf-like size, two women joined together in circumstance and coincidence.

She went to college at Oberlin with my former partner, and like me, spent numerous summers hiking in Zermatt, Switzerland. She lived in New Haven where her dad was a professor and I was a grad student at Yale, and we both went to a summer camp for lefties. Her camp was Lincoln Farm and mine was Thoreau; we competed in softball many times a season, and it's even possible that at different times we hit and caught the same ball. We have the same dishes, the same books, love the same films, embrace the connections between art and community, don't wear makeup, laugh hard and loud, work hard, are fascinated by anthropology, can be very silly, and care about helping people who can't help themselves. We each own one pair of high heels, many backpacks, and a few expensive leather pocketbooks given to us by our mothers, which we have never used. We live as members of a minority population, one in every 300,000 who have ET, a rare blood cancer.

I try to push away my diagnosis by giving concerts and lectures and by traveling internationally. She, on the other hand, lives in a beach house, focuses on growing organic vegetables, reading endless articles on health, removing stress and finding all the ways to study, understand, and deal with our disease. Reading statistics about the mortality of people with our cancer terrifies me. But she reads everything possible and makes frequent trips to specialists at the Mayo Clinic.

I discover over time that Sooze is a woman of many talents. She is a founding member of the Suquamish Museum in Poulsbo, Washington, a documentary filmmaker, oral historian, fundraiser, and medical researcher; she even rescued a historic property in Edmonds, Washington to convert it into a community arts center. She is a generous idealist whose energy and heart know no bounds.

Over the next few years, we become blood sisters who go to each other's appointments, edit each other's letters to doctors, research our cancer, and share our fears and frustrations on a daily basis. We also rage about the perils of taking care of ourselves, as doctors do not agree about optimal treatment or disease progression. We become family members who join each other's households and pass endless hours sitting around the dining room table to talk about relationships, unhealed emotional wounds, stress of family, romance, first dates, sex, afterlife, and everything under the sun. She is happily married to Al, a handsome, energetic school teacher, and I am single and reluctantly looking. She even helps with my online dating profile and, as my cheerleader, assures me that my perfect match awaits me in the not-too-distant future. Summer comes and I hike alone in remote grizzly-filled areas of the Tetons. She insists that I check in with her by phone each morning and evening so that she can track my safety. She in turn goes to the Mayo Clinic for more testing as her blood work and symptoms are worsening over time. Sooze's father was a famous statistician and she too has learned to analyze data. Even though her specialist doesn't appear to be alarmed, Sooze has been making graphs of her blood counts and, based on her declining numbers, she is certain that she is progressing to myelofibrosis, which can be deadly. She texts me daily, and one evening I am photographing a magnificent sunset when she calls and tells me important news. She will soon need a bone marrow transplant to save her life.

Blood 5
2015 – 2019—All over the world

I AM DETERMINED not to be victimized by cancer but to live a "big life" despite it. My position of Enrichment Lecturer, where I present interactive lecture performances on cruises, takes me around the world.

Sooze and I correspond on a regular basis and I feel like my trips are for both of us, kind of like a pregnant woman who eats for two. I hope that sharing my travelogues will provide her with vicarious pleasure as she awaits and then undergoes her transplant.

Dear Sooze,

Wow. Fiji is wonderful beyond my wildest dreams! Today, I kayaked to a remote village, and was introduced to a local chief in search of a new wife. After we drank some kava (please see accompanying photos of me stoned), he suggested we marry. He didn't speak English, was not really my type, and I certainly didn't feel comfortable telling him about my many girlfriends, so I had to answer with a polite "maybe."

And a few days ago I was snorkeling alone, in open water, as the others on the boat were all diving. Within my first five minutes, three large reef sharks approached me. I was terrified, and moved slowly away from them yelling up to the boat's captain, "Sharks!" He answered, "You are lucky!" Then I swam in the opposite direction and encountered three other sharks, also large. Apparently it's the season for sharks to give birth. Who knew? I shouted some expletives as I swam back to the boat and climbed out of the water. He smiled and laughed, "Today, you are really, really lucky! Relax."

A day later we had a few new arrivals at our resort. I introduced myself, "Hi I'm Amy and they interrupted, "Oh! You're the Amy we've heard about. You're the woman who swims with sharks."

Blood 6
2015 – 2019—Seattle, Washington
Doctor's Notes:

"Miss Rubin asked a litany of questions which made the exam go over time. I am recommending that she see a psychiatrist to find a way to minimize her overreactions to pain which she describes in such an inflated manner as to indicate an hysterical reaction."

"Ms. Blalock does not seem comfortable with my response to her inquiries. She insists on doing her own research, creating her own statistical analysis, and seeking out the opinions of other medical professionals which only confuses her further."

So not only are Sooze and I sick; we are also apparently downright annoying.

For my birthday, Sooze bought me a book called *Forest Bathing*, which explores the Japanese practice of shinrin-yoku or "taking in the forest."

"Is it time?"

"What time?"

"Time to stop being silent?"

"Let me check. We've only been walking in silence for six minutes and thirty-two seconds."

"So?"

"I'm not sure we'll get the full benefits unless we try to go for longer."

"Okay".

"Sooze?"

"Amy?"

"I'm getting a little tired."

"Tired of walking?"

"Of course not. Tired of not talking. I don't mind being silent when I'm in the forest alone but when I'm walking with you, there's always so much to say".

Blood 7
November 5, 2019—Seattle, Washington

WE SIT IN the exam room waiting for Dr. C. Sooze wears a protective white mask which covers her face. Her eyes are closed because of their painful burning and her breathing is ragged. She has almost no neutrophils, blood cells that protect us from infection. Most people have 5,000 and she has only eighteen, which qualifies her for the diagnosis of AML (acute myeloid leukemia). Someone else would be dead by now given her failed transplant, her multiple back fractures caused by the meds, and the fact that her bone marrow has been the battlefield of rapidly advancing cancer cells for the last ten years. She has tried every treatment available and continues to do hours of research a day to find a new answer to slow her disease progression. Every time the cancer reappears, it is stronger and moves faster to ravage the healthy cells in her body. Like a shark in a feeding frenzy, it is unstoppable.

I am trying to support her in her last stage of this disease. When I helped her into my car this morning, she whispered, "I am very sick. I am nothing like the person I was before. I'll never be that person again."

I say in a quiet voice, "I know." There is no place for me to be her cheerleader anymore or to brainstorm with her about treatments we haven't tried that wouldn't save her but might keep her alive for a few more months.

The doctor looks at Sooze's last health report and then takes a moment to compose herself. She rolls her stool back. Is she distancing herself from us? We wait to hear her words resonate in the small room where the sterile exam table is juxtaposed with batiks of exotic ladies dancing. There is no dancing for Sooze, me, or the doctor. We are past the part of the meeting that began with a joke or two and Dr. C's strangely inappropriate sharing about her former and current relationships. *Really?* Sooze and I normally rehash all the details of medical meetings and laugh ourselves silly about how crazy and dysfunctional our medical protectors are. But now is the time to focus on the elephant in the room.

Dr. C's voice is very quiet, almost like a solo flute playing a haunting melody in its lowest register. It is fragile but powerful at the same time.

"So," she takes a long breath to say what she has most likely said hundreds of times before, "Modern science and medicine have done all they can for you and your disease. We have nothing left to offer you. We have no more options." Her words are said very slowly and are not apologetic, just factual. "Yes, there could be a miracle and we always look to find hope but maybe we should be focusing now on your quality of life for the time you do have left. Perhaps it's time to consider hospice."

Sooze has asked me to take notes at this meeting. *Jesus. Am I supposed to be writing this down?* I can't read Sooze's reaction because of the mask she's wearing, but I do notice that her shoulders are slumped more than when we began the appointment. I clench my teeth and squeeze my pen to pull myself together.

I pretend I am a court stenographer recording the information quickly, efficiently, and without hesitation. At the same time, I hope Dr. C doesn't say much more. I hope she just shuts up. Sure, she's doing her job, but I don't want to hear it.

In January 2012, Dr. C had diagnosed my mother with breast cancer. I asked how much time we would have if we did nothing. "Six to nine months," she said in that quiet flutey voice. I begged my mother to fight for survival but, after struggling with three different kinds of chemo, my mom gave up and died four months later. I was actually angry at Mom for not living long enough to celebrate my 60th birthday, instead leaving me behind as an orphan with no family.

I wonder if losing Sooze will be just as terrible. Maybe if I focus on the simple tasks of making sure she is warm and nourished, maybe if I listen and protect her, maybe if I drive her to appointments, I will be able to avoid noticing how her face twitches in and out of a grimace as each breath causes her to wince. Her fingers have become spindly and her hands clutch each other to keep them from shaking. It is hard to believe that the woman sitting in front of me is not eighty but only sixty-three years old.

My friends call me "the fixer," but there is no fixing this.

Dr. C continues talking but I have stopped listening.

Somewhere in the back of my mind, buried as deeply as a dog's favorite bone, is the knowledge that I too have this disease, but I hold a different hand of cards. Mine are not yet a death sentence but more a wait-and-see roller coaster where the doctor is a master of ceremonies standing in the middle of the stage opening an envelope and reading the message inside to reveal my prognosis. Now she bends towards the microphone and makes her announcement as I hold my breath.

Blood 8

November 29, 2019—Edmonds, Washington

AL IS RUNNING back and forth, wiping surfaces with cleansers and counting out Sooze's endless pile of pills. He also bakes three kinds of fruit pies, and the smell of burnt sugar wafts in waves from the kitchen into the dining room. Sooze is sitting at the table with her son, his wife, her sister, and me. She can barely eat because her enlarged spleen, caused by the disease, is pushing against her other organs. Al hopes that even a few bites taken periodically will help restore some of the fifty pounds the disease has stolen from her. Does he really believe this?

I enter cautiously as I am not quite an invited guest. I asked permission to come over and I don't want my first introduction to a few of the most important people in her life to be after she passes.

Andy is taller than his father, muscular and, as the younger set say, "ripped." He has enormous energy that cannot be contained. He does endless pushups against the corner walls, and flexing exercises against the table. I wonder if this is his response to seeing his mother in a wheelchair. Is he doing all the movement her body can't?

Al has been baking for hours. He brings out quiches and the different pies on steaming platters. We are all smiling but we know that this will be Sooze's last Thanksgiving holiday. The talk turns to family memories. It's a game of "Can you top that," or "What could be scarier or more horrible than what I am about to share?" The winner gets more to eat.

Sooze begins, "Remember when Dad took out the inflatable kayak on the Adriatic Sea? He was whistling and enjoying the waves."

Her sister chimes in, "Yeah and he didn't hear the twenty people yelling at him to get the hell out of the water."

The sisters continue, "Remember that couple on the balcony who were pointing at him and screaming words we couldn't understand?"

"Yeah, they were saying something that sounded like "big fish" and we laughed thinking that's what Dad looked like to them—a big fish."

"Well yeah; he was a big fish in his field."

"They didn't know that." Laughter .... "And then we saw the

fin popping out of the water. We were hysterical, 'Shark, Dad, there is a shark following you,' we yelled, "but there was no reaching him. He was in his perfectly happy place, whistling and doing exactly what he wanted to be doing. It was only after he paddled to the dock that he realized Jaws was right next to him and had been chasing him for who knows how long."

Uproarious laughter which Andy joins in on. He actually stops exercising to laugh.

"And then there was the time when Uncle Harry Boner needed an ambulance but the problem was that in North Carolina they say Harry as if it were spelled "hairy." One of his kids called 911 and said, 'Harry Boner needs help. Yes, ma'am I did say that Harry Boner needs help. Ma'am … ma'am? Is anybody there?' The operator just kept hanging up on them."

More wild laughter. Sooze is the loudest and she stops playing with her quiche to add her bit. "What about our crazy cousins?"

Now her sister seems to really come to life, "You don't know the half of it. Wait, wait," the women talk over each other, breathlessly, each competing to tell their memories of horror.

"Remember—they had guns. They actually brought them to the dinner table, took them out of their holsters, and placed them right out in plain sight next to their napkins. Oh my God! We couldn't believe it! And remember, our Uncle Harry wanted to give one to Al to take home; I think it was a rifle, but Al replied, 'How am I gonna get this onto the plane?'"

More laughter. I give in to temptation and join the game even though I promised myself I'd keep a low profile. I tell them about the killer snakes I faced in Ghana: the hypnotic mambou seducing me with its translucent green color, and the cobra that we thought was a garden hose—that is, before it suddenly moved. Sounds now from all of us, part laughter, part screaming, like that crazy mix of feelings you get on a roller coaster whether you're a kid or an adult. What could be more terrifying than stories about death? Stories about almost dying, I guess.

I go into the kitchen to wash my hands again. You can't be too careful around Sooze since she has basically no immune system. "Anyone need anything from in here?" They can't even hear me as they are reliving yet another hair-raising tale.

I look out the window and imagine the boys when they were little, watching Al fry bacon and flip pancakes on Sunday mornings. He would stack plates still thick with maple syrup to be washed later, so they could run outside and jump on their sleds, screaming happily as they flew down the snowy hills that surrounded their house. Sooze adores her boys and her husband; that's totally clear.

It's very sweet but equally terrible to be here in this house, all of us together. We know that very soon she will leave us behind. We will eat pies, wash dishes, comment about the crappy weather, listen to NPR, and rage about the news, without her.

Blood 9

January 1, 2020—Seattle, Washington

I CALL THE hospital to see if she is still alive. I don't know what day it is. I'm in a panic. I'm losing my lifeline.

Sooze called me a week ago and I didn't hear the ring because I was practicing piano in my studio. Fuck the ironic timing of the universe. I barely practice these days because I spend most of my time worrying if this is the day she will die. What I wouldn't give for the chance to have had our last conversation, but no, I was busy with a task that could easily have been interrupted for something as important as our final exchange of words. The Amy-Sooze endless dialogues. And now it might be too late.

I listened to the long message she left letting me know that she was in the hospital, that her spleen was failing, and that aside from being in awful pain, which now was being managed, she was sleeping most of the time. She sounded soft and tentative, like a shy young child. She explained that she wouldn't be seeing or talking to anyone other than her family members, and that the Caring Bridge would be the best source of information about her condition. Some of her words ran together and she didn't seem to have enough air to finish her sentences. She said that she was very busy and laughed in her idiosyncratic way as if to say, "Can you believe all this is happening?"

I had been hoping to hear more from her all week long, but now I finally break down and call Al, Sooze's husband, praying that he'll answer. He does and tells me that she is back in the hospital sleeping, and that things are moving quickly in a bad direction. He says that when she wakes up, he'll call my number from her phone and put her on.

Blood 10

January 1, 2020 (a few minutes later)—Seattle, Washington
S: "Hi, is this an okay time to talk?" I'm so relieved to hear her voice, which sounds stronger than I had expected. "We're waiting

to hear if there is any hope. I'll keep trying if there is. But, I don't want this to be the new way of life. I'm ready to go at any time. I feel calm inside. I got done what needed to get done. Ordering the books for the grandson I'll never meet, and writing cards to the boys. We completed the Death with Dignity paperwork. I don't want to continue if this is how it will be." Pause. "How are you doing?"

A: "Good, really pretty good."

S: "Really?" (said like "Should I believe you?" or "Finally you're pulling it together and it's really, really, *really* taken you a while.")

A: "I'm spending time with Kate and it's going well. I feel close to her."

S: "Good."

A: "And I feel like I've been learning a lot about my stuff, my triggers and vulnerabilities. I'm making progress."

S: "You're really entering the vortex of dating." I think, Wow, vortex. What a complicated word to be saying on your deathbed.

A: "And I've been thinking about you and missing you. Missing all the stuff we've done together. Do you remember our forest bathing exercise where we were supposed to move through the forest in silence? We pretty much failed because we could only keep quiet for about six minutes."

S: "Yeah. We had many, many adventures." Now she sounds very tired.

Pause.

A: "I love you lots, you know."

S: "I love you too—pause—sometimes there's no more to say."

A: "Can I come and see you?"

S: "I'd like to see you but things change every day. Call first."

A: "Okay, I'll do that." I was surprised at how clearly she was speaking, how clearly she was thinking.

The next day I decide I should go to the hospital without delay. I pack a book to read in case she's asleep and text Al, "Is it okay for me to come now? Sooze said she wanted to see me." I wait a while for him to get back to me, and finally the phone rings.

Al says, "I got your text and was going to respond, but what I have to say should not be texted. Sooze passed away this morning."

Epilogue
January 2, 2020—Seattle, Washington

I'm SITTING AT home, alone in front of the fireplace, not quite capable of acknowledging a world without my anchor, Sooze. I think back to Spring 2015 when my disease advanced. In addition to having too many platelets, I learned I also had too many red blood cells, and the revised diagnosis of a cancer called PV. I visited Sooze at her beach house, trying to process this upsetting news. In addition to her many other talents, Sooze was a Reiki master. She gave me a healing session followed by a present of sacred stones and, finally, a worry doll to keep me safe. The next day it rained, so we browsed on Bainbridge Island where I purchased a small blue glass candle holder in the shape of a sailboat. It reminded me of our many walks and talks along the coastline in front of her house, where we dipped our toes in the water and flirted with the waves. I knew when I bought it that my precious little boat would keep me company in the days to come.

Now, five years later, I hold the worry doll against my heart.

I find myself rocking back and forth and chanting the little bits of Hebrew I know. It's likely that I'm saying the prayer for the bread, not the prayer for the dead, but really, I just don't care.

I find the precious stones she gave me and a card with the words, "You've been Forest Bathing for many years and may not have known it. But your wisdom is evident! You give me inspiration all the time. Your loving soul mate, Sooze."

It hurts too much this long dance of losing you.
Deep in my gut I am already keening.

She was one of the few people who saw me. I loved to tell her stories about my adventures. When I became frightened about my disease she would say, "Just remember, you're the woman who swims with sharks."

I make an altar in my living room by placing the stones, photos of us, books she had given me, and the worry doll in a semicircle, in the shape of a hug.

I recall something Sooze said many times in these past years. "You know, Amy, the disease is terrible but without it, we would have never met each other."

The leaves have all fallen.
The season of forest bathing has passed,

and despite my pleas I cannot freeze time or even slow its pace.

I thank my stars for the privilege and the joy of having known her.

I have walked on this path before and stopped to hug each tree, praying "Hold me with your branches and protect me now that she is gone."

I place the blue sailboat candle holder at the center of the remembrances. As I light its candle wick, I watch the flame flicker and imagine the voyage that the little boat has ahead of it, moving from now to wherever there is beyond this world.

AMY D. RUBIN is a pianist, composer, speaker, and writer. She was a Senior Fulbright Professor in Ghana and Professor of Music at the Cornish College of the Arts, Fairleigh Dickinson University, and SUNY. Amy was the Seattle correspondent for the American Center's Newmusicbox where she wrote articles about local music events and musicians. Her essay "Let it Rain" will appear in Fall 2020 in "Remembering 50," published by the Women's Leadership Initiative at Yale University.

The Long Goodbye

BY ERIC PIERRE CARTER

"ALZHEIMER'S IS DIABETES of the brain," declared my mother. It was yet another diagnosis she disclosed in her matter-of-fact way. Somehow, this bombshell fit smoothly into our conversation while we were waiting for the cornbread to finish baking in her oven.

This revelation was not a complete surprise. I had seen her memory supplements in the kitchen. For a 5'5" black woman in her early sixties, they were no more ominous to me than the vitamins and ibuprofen in the same cabinet. Arthritis, high blood pressure, diabetes, a heart stent treatment, and now Alzheimer's. Mom seemed to take each diagnosis in stride. And I tried to do the same. After all, nothing had really changed; she remained the same outgoing woman with a gift for laughter, as sharp as ever.

The previous day, I had arrived from the West Coast to visit for Christmas. While waiting for her and my suitcase at baggage claim, I felt something behind me. Turning around, I discovered my mother, smartly dressed for winter in a leopard-print beret and fur-trimmed leather coat, laid out on the airport floor, smiling up at me with her chestnut eyes like a mischievous child.

Startled and trying to stifle my laughter, I said, "What are you doing down there?"

She giggled a bit before replying, "Aren't you going to help me up?" She didn't look hurt, just a bit embarrassed.

As I helped her to her feet, she explained that she was trying to "sugar" my knees—a longstanding family prank of bumping the back of someone's knees to make them buckle. Evidently I had shifted my stance just before she bumped me. She became unsteady, and down she went instead of me, her intended victim.

Each time she told this story we would all laugh, but she made sure to cast me as the villain. "He saw his *own mother* on the floor and laughed at her. Can you believe it?"

In vain I would try to defend myself: "I was laughing because I couldn't figure out what you were doing down there on the floor."

Over the years, Mom and I typically took turns flying out to either coast, picking each other up at the airport. Sometimes on her Seattle trips she would rent a car instead and drive directly to her sister's hair salon in Tacoma or go visit some other relative. She *loved* to surprise people by coming to town completely unannounced.

After the disclosure about Alzheimer's, however, her trips to Seattle became less frequent. I didn't think much about this as I knew people's priorities and abilities change as they get older. I had seen this same pattern in my aunts and uncles.

Then in 2016 I received a frantic call from Aminah, one of my mom's neighbors who lived in the same building.

"Have you talked to your mom recently?" Aminah asked.

"Not since last weekend." This wasn't unusual. Mom and I might talk twice in a week or go a couple of weeks without chatting, so I was only mildly concerned.

"Well," Aminah said, "it's been days since anyone here has talked to her. She isn't answering the phone, replying to voicemail messages, or even responding to other neighbors who knock at her door. I also talked to her friend Margie and your mom wasn't at church last Sunday." Now I was worried. A few years earlier, Mom had passed out unconscious in her home office. Maybe she had passed out again—perhaps hours or even days ago.

There were lights on in her place and her car was in the parking lot. She hadn't told anyone that she was going anywhere with someone else. Aminah wanted my permission to have the paramedics break in. She said they couldn't figure out any other way to get inside to check on her. Now my heart was racing. I gave my permission and stayed on the line while the paramedics forced open the door. Moment by moment, I listened carefully for hopeful signs and blocked the worst possible scenarios out of my mind.

I could hear them calling to my mom as they entered her

condo. Inside, they found her napping in her bed. They woke her up and she tried to respond to some of the paramedics' questions. They checked her out but didn't find anything immediately wrong with her. Over the phone, Mom sounded alert but confused and slightly irritated by all the commotion.

Relieved for the moment but still concerned, I immediately booked a flight to the East Coast. Aminah kept a close eye on my mother until I arrived to observe her and coordinate the needed repairs to the condo door. Overall, she seemed okay. However, over the next few weeks I noticed a series of disturbing *differences* in her actions and reactions.

Opening her refrigerator to grab a snack, I could smell that something had gone off and needed to be thrown away, but I couldn't find the source. When I called my mom over to help, she claimed that she didn't smell anything bad or even unusual in the fridge. This was odd since, up till now, my mom's keen sense of smell had been the family standard. She was always the first to know if something was burning in the kitchen or if a nearby baby needed changing. Was she embarrassed and in denial about something so trivial as her sense of smell being diminished?

She had begun confusing east coast and west coast locations, such as Renton, Washington with Reston, Virginia—the sort of mistake she would have never made earlier. Also, her comprehension of the relationship between distance and travel time was slipping away, at least for relatively faraway places.

The first major thing, however, was that along with her forgetfulness she had become slightly paranoid. She avoided going to the front of the house, especially at night. Hearing voices coming from the living room and forgetting there was a TV on in there, she would ask me, "Who are those people out in the front room?" She thought that people she didn't know were staying in her house at odd hours of the night. Unknown to me at the time, these behaviors were probably indications of 'sundowner syndrome,' a pattern of agitation, fear, delusions, and wandering that often occurs in dementia patients in the late afternoon and evening.

Now my brain flipped into problem-solving mode. At the very least, she would need to be checked on regularly, possibly daily. I could stay with her until the end of month, but after that I would have to return to Seattle for work. Maybe I could arrange for Aminah and some other close friends to take turns checking on her and keeping me up to date for a while.

Riding with her to have lunch, I noticed she drove much slower than necessary, causing cars to bunch up behind her. She had always been a cautious driver, but now she was even more so. While on the road, she complained that the oncoming traffic was moving far too fast and that the running lights on the cars were bothersome and too bright. After lunch, I drove us back to the house. It was obvious that driving had become too stressful for her and that she should no longer be behind the wheel. This meant that she could no longer live in the condo by herself.

Arranging for someone to stay with her to help with grocery shopping, driving to church, the dentist, the doctor, and the like—while monitoring all of this from 3,000 miles away— would be a logistical nightmare. The choice was clear: she had to come live with me as soon as possible. Goodbye, adult independence … for both of us.

I told Mom I thought it was time for her to come back to Seattle to be with the rest of the family. For the time being, she would stay with me. Though she had a few questions, she didn't object. In fact, she seemed somewhat pleased by the prospect. I, meanwhile, felt trapped and overwhelmed. I knew that things would only become more difficult as time went on. Day by day, Alzheimer's was stealing my mother from me. And there was nothing I could do about it. Not a damn thing.

Two days before we left, I had her pack a suitcase and told her what to expect: the airport shuttles, the layover, the long second leg of the trip. Beyond that I wasn't sure how things would unfold. As much as possible, I wanted this transition to be gradual—to avoid any jarring or sudden changes. I knew that eventually Mom would need almost constant care. But I had no idea how, or even if, I would be able to afford that level of assistance for her when the time came. My only "plan" was to keep her with me for as long as I could—to care for her the way she cared for me when I was young.

On coming back to Seattle, the biggest change—as anticipated—was the abrupt lack of independence, both hers and mine. Mom could still walk to Starbucks, Walgreens, and other stores across the street from my place, but anywhere farther than that she expected to go by car. When I came home from work, she would sometimes insist on being driven to a location that she couldn't clearly describe or one that was unreasonably far away, such as a friend's house in Virginia or Texas. Telling her that I didn't know how to take her where she wanted to go seldom put her off. So, we would get in the car, drive around the city for a while, and maybe pick up groceries or dinner if we hadn't eaten yet. These 'trips to nowhere' seemed to scratch this new wandering aspect of her sundowner itch. While I found these episodes increasingly tiresome, I was grateful that it never seriously occurred to her to try getting on any of the buses that run down my street.

❧

SIX MONTHS LATER we are doing our Christmas shopping and I'm grappling with the reality of what it means to care for someone with Alzheimer's.

It took me a long time to realize that I was experiencing a long list of "lasts"—the last time she would pick me up from the airport, the last time we would go out to a restaurant together, the last time she would be asked to cook the greens for a family gathering, the last time I would help her get dressed and drive her to church ... and this, most likely, our last Christmas shopping trip together.

As her condition progressed, I constantly wondered how aware she was of what was happening to her. For me, her amazing skill with words and music and her deep insight had become taunting nostalgic recollections. I hoped she wasn't having that same experience. At one time, she traveled the world for business and pleasure. She had been to France, Italy, Japan, Guam, Hawaii, London, the Caribbean, at least 45 of the 50 states, and probably a dozen other places I've forgotten. In her retirement, I had hoped to help her add Cuba to that list. Instead, a Christmas shopping trip to Target now functions as a major adventure. I turn the car into the jam-packed parking lot.

"Wow! Look at all the people!" Mom exclaims.

Lately, Mom is continually impressed any time she sees large numbers of … anything. Cars on the freeway, crowds at a sports event, a cattle drive on a rerun of Bonanza. Anything. Is this some kind of signal I should be worried about? Does this point to a particular stage in the development of her dementia?

"It's definitely Christmas time," I say, pushing cheer into my voice. She looks excited. Concern wells up within me. "Okay, Mom, I'm going to drop you at the front door here. Go inside to get warm and wait by the door. I'm going to go park the car." I pull up to the curb and help her with the seat belt. She opens the door and crisp cool air rushes in.

"So, I'll just wait right inside the door?" she confirms.

"Yeah, Mom, I think there's some chairs and tables nearby that you can sit at. Wait for me," I repeat, "I'll be right there." I close the car door and sigh. Feeling protective, I watch her walk toward the store. She'll be fine, I reassure myself. I just need to park. I look back at her while scanning for open spots. Turning past Barnes & Noble, with her now out of view, I see an open space and slide into it.

I pop into the bookstore for a couple of minutes to look at a possible gift for my cousin, then pop back out. As I hurry to the store entrance, I try to impose my will on reality by picturing her looking for me expectantly. Making my way through the mass of shoppers, I enter Target. No mom. Still calm, I look around. Not near the entrance. Not sitting at the café area. Not looking at the jewelry or scarves. Now I'm becoming concerned.

Muscles twitch and anxiety crawls on my forehead like an invisible insect. Maybe she went to the restroom. I spin around to look in that direction, considering my options. When you're a large middle-aged black man, you don't blithely approach some unknown woman as she is coming out of a public bathroom, even to ask about someone fitting your mother's description. Hypervigilant, I decide to wait a bit longer.

The store cashiers, of course, are very busy. They probably wouldn't have noticed her unless she talked to them. It's been five minutes, but it feels like fifty. Should I have them use the PA system to ask her to meet me at Customer Service? Hearing her name called might get her to respond … I hope.

God, *please* let her be in this store.

I comfort myself by mentally listing the reasons why she has to be in this store: (1) She's especially sensitive to cold and windy weather, (2) She can't walk too far or too fast considering the arthritis in her right knee, and (3) When she gets tired, she will look for a place to sit down and return to the café area.

I can't wait here any longer; time to search the store. As I run through the aisles looking for her, I contemplate how I will explain to my aunts that I lost my mother.

After what seemed like hours, I find her looking at the Christmas decorations. These, of course, are in the corner farthest from the store entrance. She's forgotten all about meeting me by the doors. There's no point in scolding or even reminding her about our arrangement. Her pressing concern is which wreath would look best hanging on our balcony railing. Waves of relief and gratitude wash over me. We select a wreath, some lights, and a few additional presents that Mom suggests we add to our basket.

As we get into the car, Mom exclaims, "Aw, look at those little faces! They're so sweet." She makes cooing noises and waves to the children crossing the parking lot, even though they can't hear or see her through the shaded window. While looking at the kids and their families, I recall a story Mom told me.

When I was a toddler, we were heading north on I-5 towards home when I asked her where Daddy was.

"He's with his other family," she replied.

Silent for a moment, I finally responded, "That's okay, Mommy, we'll make our own family." My mother says that she drove us home wiping tears from her eyes the rest of the way.

Suddenly, we have switched positions: I am the driver and she is the passenger entrusted to my care. A half century hasn't been nearly long enough to prepare me for this new role. Passing through the streets of Seattle, it's as if five decades have vanished and taken with them local landmarks associated with fond memories that I now carry for us both.

Squeezing back tears, I recognize the truth of those words from my childhood. Yes, Mom, we did indeed make our own family.

ERIC PIERRE CARTER is a Technical Writer who suffers interminable wanderlust and *tsundoku* tendencies. A true Seattle native, he enjoys the beauty of the Pacific Northwest even on rainy days.

Do Young's Ghost

I CRAWL INTO BED, looking around my room; I feel exhausted. I have no energy for this place. I didn't clean again today. There's dust everywhere—on the floor near the walls and on all the surfaces. I'm reminded of things left undone: books half read, projects unfinished, and laundry piling up. Living alone makes it challenging to keep up with it all, and it's easy for me to berate myself. These thoughts make my shoulders and neck tighten up. My body wants to rest. I feel tired after a long day. I'm single, I'm alone.

Pulling up my blankets, I conjure his ghost. And he is here with me now, my Do Young. The pillow becomes his arms, the blankets his strong legs. Those arms and legs wrap me up, like they did in life. Sighing heavily, I accept his love for me. Remembering his smooth chest and body and how I used to run my hands down his strong, muscled legs and ass, enjoying his lack of hair. Invigorated by his strength, I drift along in this fantasy. Even now, after so many years, he excites me and I allow myself to be aroused. As usual, I let him take the lead.

He roughly says, "I want you, Gigi"—his nickname for me. His breath smells a little of garlic. His energy surrounds me. His passion apparent and strong. He was always passionate with me. I push into the pillow, imagining he's on top of me. Imagining he enters me; I accept him here with me. My body stirs as it always does when I'm with him. My heart speeds up and my breath deepens.

"Do Young," I whisper back. "Remember what a perfect match we were? You were the first one for me."

"Yes, Gigi, I remember," he whispers. His face is on my neck, his breath warm. I feel his body quiver as he takes deep breaths. His breath is my breath, deep and quickening.

"I'll stay with you, Gigi," he says, and this time I believe him. These are the words I want to hear. I relax and my breathing slows. He's with me and has nowhere else to go. We hold each other tightly and I begin to fall asleep. I'm home; he's with me again tonight. I can sleep soundly.

As I relax and begin to fall asleep, the familiar questions pop into my head: "Why did you cheat on us?" My chest tightens a little, and I'm less relaxed, alert yet still sleepy. I wait to hear his answer. "Why didn't you tell me that you were no longer being monogamous? Why did we stop using condoms? Why did I stop protecting myself?"

We knew HIV was a possibility. I thought I was safe. I

sense myself holding my breath; there's anger mixed with disappointment.

I remember finding his briefcase unlocked, nearly thirty years ago. It was sitting in the usual spot, and every now and then, when I felt an extra tinge of suspicion, I'd see if it was locked. And, it was always locked. But not this time, incredibly, this morning the case was unlocked. With shaking breath and hands, I looked in and saw the envelope from the photo developing company. And there inside are photos of a young man sitting on our couch, in our living room; he isn't naked or in a sexual pose, just sitting there looking totally comfortable on my couch, in my home. Like he'd been there several times before.

"Why, Do Young?" He doesn't answer me. Yet he still holds me. I begin sighing and taking deep breaths. I feel deflated, helpless, useless. I allowed myself to be used, to be treated so poorly. He continues holding me.

"Gigi," he whispers. "I didn't take good care in our relationship. Forgive me, please. I'm sorry." He grips me tighter; I feel his strength. Passively, I relax in his arms, allowing myself to be fully held.

"At least now I know where you are and no longer worry about who you're with." I can trust you now. I know you love me. Yet now I'm HIV positive, and tired, feeling old and socially rejected.

With these thoughts stirring in my mind, I continue, "Why didn't you tell me you were dying, Do Young? How come I had to find out about it on Facebook?" A post saying simply, "We lost our friend Do Young today; he lost his battle to cancer."

The last time we spoke you sounded tired but you didn't tell me the cancer had returned. I cry out loud, feeling helpless. Lost. I'm alone in this pain. He's gone. I let myself break down and sob, my body shuddering, my nose running.

After crying, I begin again to fall asleep. I look forward to dreaming. In my dreams I'm pain free. No longer weak and heavy, no longer lonely. I'm connected to the world. Energized and engaged. Sometimes I even fly!

In the morning, Do Young's gone. I'm glad there's no one here to see me now. Most mornings I wake in pain. Joint, body aches, headache, and weakness. For more than twenty years nearly every day I am in pain. Waking slowly, sighing heavily, I try to get comfortable.

My chest heaves and I take some deep breaths. I don't scream or hit anything but I want to. I have no control over this pain, only how I respond to it.

Rolling onto my back, I begin to do Reiki on myself and there is an immediate shift.

My breathing relaxes and I am calmer. My joints are less stiff and sore, reminding me that things change, that even this pain passes.

Sometimes whole days are filled with physical pain. Arthritis pain. Dizziness. I think I have fibromyalgia but there's no diagnosis. I'm told that this is HIV disease. Exhausted from these days, at night I just want someone to hold me. I want to feel less alone.

Suddenly feeling defiant, I decide to conjure Do Young during the day. Despite the pain, physical and emotional, I decide to go out. I grab my coat and smile knowing that my ghost will go with me. I feel hungry and have a craving for Korean food. I guess that's what I'll eat for lunch.

GREG COLUCCI is a storyteller, is HIV+ and has Huntington's Disease, a genetic, neurologic, progressive illness – meaning symptoms will increase with time. He is honored to consider himself an elder of his community and has many stories he wants to share.

Aloneness

BY CHRIS DOELLING

I CLOSE MY FRONT door on the ashen twilight sky and its accompanying winter rain. I cannot say my apartment is particularly warm, not yet. It is dry, however, and once I flip on the gold light familiar objects greet me in my crammed one-bedroom apartment. My shoulders relax as I exhale.

I am home earlier than expected because my writing buddy cancelled last minute. It was one of two social engagements I make myself go to per week. I know I need these in order not to lose touch with the human world and to keep my social skills from getting too odd and awkward. I try not to be too happy about one less obligation.

I think back to fifteen years ago. I left the therapist's office; it was my last visit because I was about to liquidate my life and travel abroad for at least a year as a backpacker. In therapy, we had just unpacked that I had interpersonal trauma from my childhood. She explained that for me it meant trust issues and not feeling safe or stable in relationships.

I shrugged and said, "Well, I guess it's something I will have to unpack while on the road." She assured me with a glint in her eye that it would take years to really work through it all. The implication was that without therapy, which I was now giving up for my journey, I would never really work through it. And perhaps she was right.

Back in my living room, I fling my raincoat over the Moroccan lamp hook and my down coat over my bike rack, covering up other items already hung there. I slip off my wet hiking boots with a thud against the front door. Damp socks land nearby. No one else will need to stumble over them—because I live alone.

Alone. Maybe I took the pact I made with myself at twenty-three a bit too seriously. I remember running into my ex unexpectedly in the new town where I had just moved to finish a degree long postponed in part because of him. That was the age before we had the word 'codependency' as parlance in our culture or charts about cycles of abuse to reference while waiting for our gynecological exams at Planned Parenthood. That was an age like all the ages before where we fumbled blindly through relationships without a tool bag or knowledge of what 'healthy' meant.

I saw him across the street—warmth sprang up in me; he was still cute. He had muscled up again and his hair was growing out; I liked it better long. He had the familiar satyr smile on his Italian lips. I felt the resolve in me weaken. The scar itched from where he had hit me on the forehead a year earlier. We talked briefly. He seemed surprised to hear I was going back to college, as if he thought he could stop me, perhaps. He was flattering at first, telling me I looked good.

I had staved off his beautiful letters for weeks. At first I had read them and admired the artwork he drew in the margins. The letters were full of love for me and full of all the self-improvements he'd made. Still, I stopped reading the letters after a while. The tone had shifted; there was more anger in them as they progressed. I did not throw them out, but I didn't read.

Now in front of me, I realized he was eyeing the sweater. I wanted to hit myself upside the head. It was his sweater: cotton knit, all stretched out. It had served me well through my living out of a car in our Deadhead days. It was blue plaid on top and plain beige on the bottom with an overall dingy tone from too much wear and washing.

"You still wearing that?" he asked. Those flexible lips now had the lift of a sneer on the left.

The loosening of my boundaries that had occurred as we talked, all the softening in my heart, ceased. The internal lockdown started. I couldn't hide the flash of pain in my face. I shrugged. All the jabs of his derision, the surgical precision of his flaw-finding, came back to me. Four and a half years I tried being in that relationship. I had every emotion I thought I could have; not knowing my own boundaries, I had given it my all, which was too much. At twenty-three I was exhausted. I felt like I had lived it all with him. Within that moment I made a vow to never throw so much of myself away again—not for anyone.

That resolve might have stuck too well.

I shake the memory off. It's been over half a lifetime now. I smile sadly at the memory of how I was never as old as I was when I was twenty-three.

Still in my living room, I look at the wire mesh shelving that holds canvas bins full of art supplies, the ancient school desk cluttered with sewing machine and bins full of paintbrushes and other craft detritus. The bookshelf is mostly covered by various sizes of canvases tilted against it from that time I tried to take photos of my artwork. When was that, three months ago now? I've not put anything away. Unlike my partnered friends, there is no one to squabble with over unfinished projects that lie around forever. Guilty pleasure wells up inside me. My mess, mine, mine, mine.

No one's been over in a year. I go to my friends' houses instead; my excuse is the clutter and "Hey, I am trying to live in the same space as my art studio and I just don't have enough room for both."

My thoughts lock on the last time I really went through all my belongings, putting them away in boxes. I was packing up for that same long trip abroad after my therapist had enlightened me about my relational patterns. I had just gotten a call from my ex. I thought I was older and wiser then at forty-four. But no. This ex had been a roller coaster ride. I had been the new addition in an unsuccessful poly relationship. Although it was very fashionable to be poly in the queer community I found myself in, it didn't work for most of my acquaintances who tried—though I know it works for others. I saw a lot of jealousy and one partner dragging the other into opening things up.

I could see it and yet, because I was too attracted, I could not pull myself out. Even on our last date, we were in the middle of making out when their primary partner called. Calling was something I wasn't supposed to do when they were together. They spent an inordinate amount of time on the phone; I might as well not have been there. It had rankled but I'd known it was the end. Thankfully, the trip was the artificial constraint I needed to get out of yet another epic bad choice I had made in love.

I recall those last few days before my trip. My ex, on the phone, had just told me they loved me, and I felt it; I felt a love that wasn't there; I knew the words were hollow. It's not that they were heartless; they just were too preoccupied with their own needs. Intellectually they would like to love me, but theoretical love isn't a great substitute for the real thing. Just as, theoretically, they thought they could do a poly relationship. I knew all this, but emotionally I could feel the warm plastic of my phone radiating love at me. Was I only giving myself permission to feel love? Did I really have to go through this circus to find myself alone among my moving boxes finally feeling love? Couldn't I cut out the intermediary and feel this love for myself?

❧

TEN YEARS LATER and emotionally free from even a lingering regret, I light a candle and a stick of incense. I smile at my makeshift altar corresponding with the season, spring, a green ring of artificial moss pebbles and artificial daisies, one of my abstract mandala paintings in the background. It is sky blue to align with the clearer, warmer skies that are beginning to approach.

Being alone is healing for me. The therapist all those years ago was right—I have a low-grade anxiety around other human beings. I cannot be at ease completely; my ear is always pricked for potential problems that I need to be alert to.

Back in high school, I had the dawning knowledge that I could have some modicum of control over my environment if I could just plan for it. I would wake up two hours before everyone else in the family so that I could roam the lower parts of the house alone. I also remember my hands constantly shaking while living in that house. I would putter around the kitchen making weak Folgers coffee and roaming freely through the den. And I could keep my bedroom door open, ever vigilant for signs of stirring above. When I heard sounds, I would slink back into my room, close the door and lock it.

I remember after my first year away at college looking at my hands in the morning and realizing they no longer shook.

Now in my apartment, I hear the murmuring of my downstairs neighbors through cardboard-thin floors. I try to walk light-footed when I hear them. Still a vigilance remains, but minor, easily dismissed because I have my own space with a lock on a door that is much stronger. Nobody comes to jiggle and jiggle it. I am safe.

At sixteen, I worked in a convalescent center. My job was to do activities with the patients there. Because I was the new kid, the inexperienced one, they put me in the back rooms. This meant that I worked with the elderly who were no longer lucid, most of them spending their days in a wheelchair, sleeping or staring blankly out the windows. No one visited them. Occasionally I got to chat with the folks in the front room who still knew their names. Even they received few visitors. There were always excuses, like the too-busy lives of their family members. It seemed so unfair. Not that I knew the individual stories, but these surviving mostly women had been married, had owned houses, had done everything they were supposed to, including raising children. Yet here they were forgotten and waiting for the inevitable. Some with sharp minds and poor health and some with no memories at all. There was no guarantee, even when you followed social norms, that you would not in the end find yourself alone and forgotten at some care facility.

As I reflect, I pour myself some orange juice and thin it with water, refreshing but not too sweet. I take a sip. I remember articles about forgotten elderly people who pass away in their apartments unnoticed sometimes for days.

And how:

Millennials are lonelier than ever.

Also:

Therapists warn about social isolation and the harm that feeling isolated and alone can have on physical and mental health.

The message repeatedly is that being alone is a problem. It is even harmful.

I stick a black licorice wheel in my mouth. I don't even unwind it to chew on the individual strands, something about the mouth feel. Chewing it thoughtfully, I take another sip of my watered-down beverage. Orange juice tastes somehow more orange after licorice.

I think about my travels in India and Nepal. How I learned quite the opposite lesson about being alone. I met spiritual seekers; and dharma community recognized gurus who intentionally withdrew from society for decades. They chose to be alone to fully embrace their practice. The repeated point here was to fully walk the spiritual path one needed to spend time renouncing the world. Ultimately, returning to the world would test your realizations, and if you could teach others, you should. But many spend their remaining days in simple huts and even caves.

I also learned that in the Tibetan Buddhist tradition the journey into death is best undertaken away from clinging to mourning relatives who make it hard for you to let go. Better to take this journey in a quiet place without distraction.

These ideas contradicted so sharply what I'd been taught by the society I came from that they rattled my perceptions about loneliness. It made me reexamine everything I thought I knew about being alone. It also gave me permission to ask questions and, against therapist recommendations, to view loneliness and isolation as something perhaps useful, in my case even a remedy.

I cannot pinpoint whether it is something maladaptive in me that forced the path of aloneness I now tread—or was it always a secret wish to be a bit apart from others? To be solo so that I could really sink into my own skin and mind without being roused out of my introspections? What if this being alone was for me actually a balm, a remedy for all those strong emotions I can feel when overwhelmed by social confusion? Perhaps it did not start out as a choice, but now I choose it.

I turn on my ancient MP3 player whose battery life is now less than two hours. I plug in the earbuds and I turn on my dance list. The window shades are all snugly drawn; the neighbors do not need to see or hear me—except perhaps the footfalls of my now bare feet on the carpet as I do my combo bellydance-hula-hippie hiphop and other made-up dance styles. I move around in the three-by-eight-foot cleared rectangle in my living room.

I dance out the day's tension; I dance out the self-conscious embarrassments of what if anyone saw me, a fifty-three-year-old goof. I let go of the tightness in my hips. I forget myself and work out the kinks in my shoulders. I am wholly in my body; I come to an alert consciousness and am full of satisfaction and joy. I surprise myself again at my ability to sink into such fearless abandon.

Loneliness and solitude have become a blessing.

CHRIS DOELLING has lived and traveled overseas a fair bit and has also called Seattle home for about thirty years now. Working towards earning the title "Elder," Chris has been amassing experience and is now processing these experiences to continue to grow, learn, and heal, and to share any gems that can be pulled out of the mud.

Twenty-Third Street

BY NANCY KIEFER

YOU KNOW WHEN someone wants to give you something? You have to be there to receive it, right? And to receive this thing, your hand has to be open. It can't be the hand that is covering a wound to the chest, one that is putting pressure on that wound; it has to be wide and ready. The fingers and thumb must be held lightly, the palm turned up.

I was seventeen years old when I was put on a train. I took with me my teenaged husband of two days, my daisy-flowered luggage, my hipster trench coat, my morning sickness, my cigarettes, a neatly packed shoebox of sandwiches and cookies my mother put together, my Illinois driver's license, and the linen dress with the Nehru collar I had worn to the chapel where the family had reluctantly gathered to endure the wedding ceremony. (In the photos of that day, my parents look as though they are slightly tilted away from us).

The collar on that dress hid a necklace of hickeys Freddie had placed on my neck a few days before the wedding. The hickeys had faded by the time the train arrived in Yakima. Yet, in this single anecdote, which I have told over the years, I am only revealing the part of the story that I have always told. I tell it as though it were not me in that dress, but a girl in a funny story who happened to have my name.

August 1970

SHE WAS WASHING the dishes and I was drying. The kitchen was bright with sunlight. It seemed like she was washing the same dish over and over.

"Mom?" I said.

"What?" There was a strong *t* sound at the end of her question. I tried to form words.

"Mom?"

"You're pregnant," she said. Her flat tone told me she had suspected this for some time.

"Yeah…," I whispered.

She rinsed her hands but she didn't look at me.

"I figured that."

Was that the same plate or a different plate I was drying? There was no talking for a long time. The smell of suds.

"Well, just what are you going to do?" she said, in an accusing voice that belied the helpless gesture of her hands. I had seen her throw her hands up like that many times. And what *was* I going to do? I had just finished eleventh grade and I had not been allowed to stay out after 11:00 p.m. My parents and teachers had pretty much told me what to do. I only knew how to break rules while living safely under the rules.

"Because your dad says, and I agree … you can't live here."

She stared at the faucet, then rinsed the spoons. I heard my father's voice in this decision. When she was obeying what he said and didn't really believe in it, she spoke in a higher octave, with hesitant spaces between words.

What had I hoped for? Not this. I wanted to ask her for love. I wanted to beg. Instead, a crushing self-hatred overtook me and in this shame I felt certain I had gotten what I deserved. I had made my bed and now I would lie in it.

A long string of reminders I had heard since I was a little girl came to me. I understood that not only had she suspected my unwed pregnancy, she had been tracking it down, as if it were always waiting for me. *A pretty girl like you better watch out. Don't find yourself in trouble. You will have a nice life if you don't end up PG like so and so.*

I stood next to her, my bare feet on the scrubbed linoleum, while we finished the dishes. I may have looked like I was there, but inside I was somewhere else falling off a tall building. I was no more than a piece of paper turning in the wind.

"I don't know, Mom. I don't know what I am going to do."

I was suddenly very lonely. I was glad she was turned from me so she could not see tears pooling in my eyes. I hated tears. I vowed that she would never see me cry again for as long as I lived.

"Well," she said, holding up two fingers and looking directly at me, "You have two options. You can marry Freddie or you can go on ADC."

I had lots of friends living in the housing projects who received Aid to Dependent Children. My parents never approved of my friends and made it clear that the projects were a dangerous and unclean place to visit. In their eyes, the worst thing was to "end up" on ADC. It meant a life of dirtiness, fighting, snot-nosed little kids, hoodlums, and drunken mothers with cigarettes hanging out of their mouths. I had found this all somewhat exciting. But it was not lost on me that they preferred me to go live there instead of staying in our house.

"And you can forget about finishing high school. Your life ... let's face it ... it is ruined." Her hands flew up in the air again.

The kitchen was so cheery. Cherry patterns on the curtains, ironed. I wanted to say something, but nothing would come to my mouth. She squeezed out the dishcloth and hung it on the hook. I remember hearing a cupboard shut. On the table, the radio was playing Aretha. She snapped it off.

First Amends - 1997

WE WERE TALKING over coffee when the subject of my moving away so many years earlier came up. Suddenly it got really hot in the room. I started to sweat. Inside I was begging, *Don't say anything, Mom.*

I quickly jumped into a funny story that I hoped would hijack this painful one we never discussed, the one that was like a giant hand pushing us apart yet holding us together by its touch.

"Mom," I said, gearing up to talk fast and make her laugh,

"Did I tell you about the first Thanksgiving I had in Yakima and how I mistook a bowl of green chilis for green beans?"

This hijacking was a common practice in our family when cornered by an uncomfortable subject. We used humor to exit a conversation. She often started it, or willingly played along, but this day she was not having any of it.

She shifted in her chair. "I'm serious. How did you ever make it, Nancy?" She hunched her shoulders and flung her hands in the air, palms up, to accentuate that question. "I can't imagine it. I've always been so afraid to do new things."

"Oh, I was lucky, I guess, Mom. It probably made me stronger." I showed her my muscles. Did I do new things? She made this sound like an adventure I chose to go on. *You sent me off, remember?*

Boxers sniff back the blood. I watched a lot of boxing movies in those days. *Keep it light. We have come so far in the last twenty-five years. Don't blow it by being mushy.* But I was less afraid of being mushy than I was of remembering things that made me die inside: the shame of my pregnancy, my broken marriage, the train ride two thousand miles away with fifty dollars in our pockets. And her absences: Giving birth to my beautiful boy without her, all the major events in our lives without her. I told myself it made me tough as nails. Nails secure things tightly but they bend if you pull them out wrong. I was tough, but not tough enough to face this torn-up place in my gut.

"Now, Nancy listen to me. I need to say this," she said. I flinched. "Nancy, I am so sorry we ever sent you away like that. I regret that decision to this very day. I regret I was not stronger.

I regret I could not stand up to your dad."

I could not allow a long silence. I jumped quickly in to reassure her all was A-OK.

Okay, so I was not exactly important to Dad. I knew that. But she gave me away and she lost us, me and my boy. Honestly, I thought I somehow deserved it. Now I didn't want to rock the boat because I was finally getting close to her again. What if everything fell apart and she took away her love again?

"Forget it, Mom. It all turned out for the best. It was what it was. I made it okay. You gave me a lot of those midwestern survival skills," I said too loudly. If the joking didn't work, maybe flattery would.

To myself I said, *Stop, stop, everything is all right, it is all right for fuck's sake. I have survived and I am here with you, and you finally love me and I surely love you, and let's just shut the hell up about it and let's just rock this life as it is.*

She turned away, looking down at her hands as if something weird was happening to her fingers.

"No. No, it's not all right," she said softly. I let out a breath.

"Let's have more coffee," I crossed my arms.

"Okay," she said." And that was that.

Wedding Day - September 1970

ON THE MORNING of my wedding, I had two stomach aches. The aches were distinctly different yet interchangeable, fitting into each other as if they were a set of oversized twins. The first was milky, full of bees, and it made me squint my eyes hard, then open them wide. That was the *Is- This- Really- Happening* stomach ache. The second was a familiar nausea that had been rising in my throat for weeks; it was the ache that told me firmly that I was pregnant.

I looked around my bedroom. The dress, the good one with the Nehru collar, was hanging primly on a hanger in my empty closet. It wasn't a wedding dress, and I had bought it on sale a year before but, unlike most of my clothes, it had some feminine aspects to it. It did have a little purple food stain on the sleeve, but I figured it would be fine as long as I kept the small bouquet of flowers in front of it during the picture taking. As I got up from the bed, I put my hand on my sheets. *Would I see these sheets again? Should I put them in my suitcase?* I didn't want to leave them. So many things I did not want to leave behind. The day before, I had packed most of the essentials, leaving my hippie-mod bedspread and the peace sign collage I had decoupaged. It was harder to leave the true and precious objects I owned and loved. The ones I had found in grade school by exploring or riding my bike around Rock Island—the mysterious earth-stained metal bear I had dug out of the ground with a stick, a bowl of broken cat eye marbles, fancy rocks of all sizes (could be gold), and all the musty ledgers and old leather notebooks I had scavenged from digging in my ancient neighbor's garbage bin after he died.

Lined up against the wall were the cardboard boxes my mother and I had packed the day before—a book by Hemingway from my brother (hadn't read it), winter clothes (what's the weather in Yakima?), a set of green sap-colored pots and pans my father gave me (he got them free), embroidered pillowcases and doilies from a girlfriend at the makeshift baby shower given for me the week before. *How many boxes were we taking on the train? Maybe eight? Where was the flowered cloth-covered suitcase I was going to carry with me on the train?* I panicked. *There it was. There it was.*

To calm myself, I imagined the itinerary for the day. In one hour, I was going to the chapel to be married. First I would take a bath, then I would put that dress on and comb out my long blonde hair after pulling out the giant prickly curlers. Then I would cover my cheeks with liquid blush and put on the green creamy eye shadow or maybe the pearlescent. I'd use black mascara, and finally the whitish-pink lipstick. After that I would squirt myself with something from Avon, probably Honeysuckle. I would come downstairs where my parents and my sister would be already dressed and waiting to drive to the church.

At the chapel, we would meet Freddie, his cousin Ricardo, and his Aunt and Uncle. We would exchange the rings Mom bought for us. After that we would have sandwiches and potato salad and ice tea served back at the house with some guests, and finally Freddie and I would spend the night at the Sheraton Hotel in downtown Rock Island as husband and wife. I had the sequence memorized but I had no idea what any of it meant, whether I was a real person or just one talking to myself in a cloudy dream. A big part of me was perched far away, in a high tree, with my wings folded and my eyes shut.

Train - 1970

MY DAD HAD already loaded the eight boxes into our car by the time Freddie and I returned from our honeymoon night at the

Sheraton. I found it funny that we stayed in a room I had actually cleaned many times, having worked there for several summers as a maid. The sun had not come out yet and the Illinois humidity put a shine of sweat on my skin. My flowered suitcase stood by the back door.

I hung on to the belief that this train trip, this moving to the state of Washington with Freddie, leaving my house, my school, my neighborhood, my bedroom, my teachers, my friends, and especially my little sister, was not going to happen. I believed that my mother would have to stop this part of the movie; she would refuse to buy the tickets, demand that I stay close to home. My mother would put her foot down; she would say to my father, in front of me, protecting me, that enough is enough, and they both would then ground me, ground both Freddie and me. I wanted to throw myself on the ground, at their feet, and beg them to beg me to stay. I was close to fainting from this hope. I thought briefly that at least if I fainted they would have to take care of me and we would not be going on the train. All these ideas ran through me as we gathered the rest of my things and walked out to the car. Yet, I knew my face was inscrutable, like a bowl of milk reflecting nothing. They would not beg me to stay and they could not know how much I wanted them to stop me from leaving. It was our family way of doing things.

The drive to the station in the neighboring town of Savannah was quiet. My sister, only ten, was silently fiddling with a button on her blouse. Freddie was looking down at his wedding ring, twisting it. I held my head in one position, moving my eyes left and right but not saying much.

When are you going to stop the car? My guts were churning and both stomach aches were in full force. I said nothing. As we got closer to the train station, my dream of them turning the car around lost all its color, became brown and gray.

We gathered on the platform, waiting to board. We did not know what to say to each other. My mother tried some light talk, some jokes that fell flat. She handed me fifty dollars and I put it in my purse; then she tried to jokingly say, "Write us when you get a job." I did not pretend to laugh because I believed that to be true. We earned our money or we went without in our family. My sister cried. My father looked away. He was often very quiet and there was not a way for me to read him. I suspected he was behind all this, but yet it was my mother who was breaking my heart.

I didn't have words for my feelings. I didn't have a mouth for words. I just knew that right then I wanted the train to arrive immediately so we could take ourselves away from them.

Tears were trying to fill my eyes but I made them turn back. With stiff little waves that reminded me of how we said goodbye to our aunt when we were leaving Grandma's funeral, Freddie and I climbed the steps and entered the train.

Letters to Home - June 15, 1971
Dear Mom and Dad,

Hi there! I can't believe that Nicky is already two months old. He is using the pacifier you sent in the package. He has already outgrown those little tee-shirts! He is so cute I can't believe it. Everybody here calls him Booboo.

I am working two mornings a week cleaning house for this rich German lady. She is really (underline, underline) picky. She hired me over the phone. I don't think she likes that I am such a German. She said on my first day that she thought I was going to be a Mexican girl because of my last name and that all her friends have Mexican cleaners so she wanted one too. Oh well.

Anyway, we are really excited to come and visit you in August. We are going to stop in Pullman first, drop off our stuff at the apartment, and then drive straight to Illinois. Then we will come back to Pullman, unpack, and then Freddie will start school. I can't wait to come! Nicky will be four months old by then! He just gets cuter and cuter.

The Batmobile (Dodge Polara) is in pretty decent shape because we bought it from a little old lady who hardly ever drove it. It will definitely get us there.

See you soon!

Love xxxxxxxxxx

Nancy and Frederico and Booboo

My heart was beating hard thinking about this trip to Illinois. I had not seen my family since the wedding and now I would be coming home with a darling, adorable boy. I couldn't wait to show them this creature who was so loved by my new family in Yakima, cooed at and held and hugged and laughingly baby-talked to in the most ridiculous of goofy voices by tias, uncles, cousins, and the huge clan of extras (like me) who became part of the family. I was putting the money from my cleaning job into a secret drawer to pay for gas.

I, like my boy Booboo, felt as though I had come as an infant and been given the nurturing gift of acceptance and love by the women in Freddie's family. Just as loss had slipped inside me on the train, this radiant love also slipped inside me. I received it without knowing. My new sisters and my new mother were the first women outside of my family I had fallen in love with. It was not a lesbian love, of course; it was a love that tied me to women as the harbors of trust for the rest of my life.

For reasons I fully accepted as normal at the time, my mother had not come to Yakima for the birth of the baby. She did not know that I spent my labor calling *Mommy, Mommy* or that someone (was it a nun?) had frequently come by and stroked my forehead, telling me I was going to be okay and whispering to me, "Look at your skin. You are just a little girl."

Letters Home - August 27, 1972

DEAR MOM,

How is everything going? Hope it's not too hot in Illinois.

Everything is not so fine here. I might as well tell you that Freddie and I are going to split up. It's sort of hard for me to be objective about the reasons but the fact is he's not really ready to settle down and be a good husband. He provides for us, but that's not enough for me. I need someone to stay home and not run around with other girls. I think I've forgiven him enough times for adultery that I've become restless and nervous myself. When I stand up to him he gives me some nice contusions and then I have to tell everyone I ran into the refrigerator.

I would have told you a year and a half ago but I didn't want you to worry and I thought if I just keep quiet and keep trying it will stop. I've finally gotten enough guts and confidence to do what has to be done. I've tried ultimatums, marital counseling, and now, for the last six months, I've just become apathetic and impossible to live with. I have been frigid for a long time now. He calls me a frigid bitch. I don't want to end up a bitter old bag.

I still feel guilty for leaving but that is because I am sorry it didn't work out. I'm not ready to be with anyone else, I just need to be alone and get my head together.

You know Mom, when I thought of writing to you I only thought I'd write a few rigid sentences but here I am spilling my guts out. All this has been tucked inside me for a long time and now I am letting it out. I've been a phony and all my "I am fine" is "bullshit" and I'm not happy-go-lucky all the time. And you knew it, didn't you!

I guess I can't be "the girl who got married young and made it anyhow." I guess you do understand. I don't have anyone else to tell this to. All my friends and family here are Freddie's.

I'm still going to try and go to school this fall. If you sign this paper enclosed then I will be able to apply for financial aid. I want to make something of myself. I plan to stay here but I do know that if it doesn't work out I could come home? I'd work my butt off at a job and I won't ask you for any handouts at all. I won't be a big baby like Uncle Bob's daughter. Also, you see, it won't do me any good to depend on you after depending on Freddie because then I will never become a mature woman.

I want the best for Nicky so I have to get a degree. I think Nicky will do better with just one parent who loves him rather than two who fight all the time.

Well, I better go. I'm not going to rewrite this or I will tuck everything back inside myself. It's just time for me to be honest with myself for once.

Love to you all,

Nancy and Nicky

PS See below for my new address starting in September.

August, 1973

Dear Mom and Dad,

I hope it is not too hot there. It is super hot here. The wheat fields are being harvested and at night the air is all cloudy with wheat.

After we came back from the visit with you, I found out that I will be getting less financial aid for the school year than I thought. Freddie is not paying the child support. Luckily, my rent is super cheap. I think I may need to borrow twenty dollars this month and I will be able to pay it back by September 16th, which is when the financial aid and student loan check can be picked up at the college. I am applying for a grant and that will cover us. I also applied for a job to make ends meet at this tavern downtown but they said I had to be twenty-one to work there. Maybe next year.

Meanwhile, Nicky is doing pretty good, I think. He has learned a new way to scream that sounds really scary but he laughs when he does it. It is so hilarious. Ha-ha. They're Coming to Take Me Away haha! Remember that song? That's how hilarious it is when he screams.

Talk to you soon,
Love and xxxxxxxx
Nancy and Nicky

I drew daisies on the top of the letter and made a cartoon of Booboo screaming and me covering my ears. (She'll get a kick out of that.) Then folding the letter neatly in threes, I put it in the envelope and carefully placed the stamp on it so it would not be crooked. (They wouldn't like crooked.)

Nicky was in his high chair practicing that new sound again—a high pitched scream. He paused for a minute to relish the noise he was making, then screamed louder. I loved his cute little face and the big smile he had, even though the screaming made me feel crazy. I looked for my Dr. Spock book; maybe there was something about screaming. *Was it normal? Who to ask?* I didn't know very many mothers. Everybody was a coed in Pullman. I didn't want to ask any questions at the university in case somebody would think I was a bad mother. Happy, married people didn't have screaming loud kids, right? Or if they did, it didn't bother them, right?

I knew she would send me the money and she would say, "Don't mention this to your dad." That rule had been going on since childhood. If she bought my sister and me school shoes in September, she would say, "Don't mention this to your dad." I also knew, because I came from a "no-handout" family, that I would send that money I borrowed from her the day I received it from the financial aid office.

Memory is a funny thing. There are the things you think

you remember, the perceptions of reality you are convinced you understand, and then there is the reality. I would have never believed I wrote those letters to my mom if I had not found them in an envelope with my name on it after her death. My perception was that I kept all feelings to myself, that I wrote only daisy-covered notes that told nothing about myself. Yet, in these letters, I found evidence that I had called upon my mother, especially upon her, many times in my early years. She kept an envelope of my happy cards and evidently, I discovered later, an envelope of my earlier more "troubling" letters. When did I start hiding myself?

1993

"This round of chemo isn't going so hot, Nance," my mother's tired voice said on the phone.

This was my father's third bout with what the doctor had called "curable cancer." He was on the mend, but the pain of radiation in his throat and the doses of chemo had left him hurting and exhausted.

"He's just miserable. Miserable, and we can't seem to find anything that will help him."

Her use of 'we' was usual, and I knew she was feeling his pain as if it were her own.

"Mom, now sit down for a minute. Tell me how I can help you." I had learned a lot of new language in my faculty job at the college women's center. It made me sound obnoxious, but I hadn't realized it yet.

"Nancy, just let me sit awhile; just let me get myself together," she said with some irritation.

"Okay, I am here mom." Chastened, I stayed quiet and let her do what she needed to do. We were silent a long time.

"Ah, all better now. Thanks for letting me just sit here," she said, her nose still stuffy from crying.

I was surprised at how well I was responding to this. Somehow had I become mature? If so, when did this come about? It was true that over these years we *had* grown in our admiration for each other. Not just my mother, but my father as well. I didn't think I was exactly loved, but I accepted this more as a reality that would not change. I equated maturity with letting go of childish dreams. Though we still lived 2,000 miles apart, we kept in touch weekly at least.

"Okay, Nance. I will call you in a few days and check in with you about Daddy."

"Love ya, Mom. Give my love to Dad." I knew I would call her the next day. I had been calling them every day for the last few months.

But still, I hoped, and it wasn't something I was proud of, that this new maturity and attention to them would … uh … *make me the preferred one.* I fantasized for a minute about how this could play out. My mother would be describing my unusually good helpfulness to her friends, saying with sincerity, "We sent her away, and yet … and yet, she was the one who came through for us."

That teenaged girl was always with me, invisible yet operating behind the scenes with as much finesse as she could muster. *Make me feel loved. See me.* This orphan seemed to exist without my permission.

"Before I hang up, how's the kid, Nancy?" Mom had a second wind.

My son was now in his twenties and spending his time going to community college, dating girls, and working at a steak house. He was doing okay for the time being. A smart kid with some major learning issues, he had had a choppy ride at times.

"He's being himself." I smiled. He certainly was an individual, and stubborn in his politics and attitude. He had defied me on all ends. Raising him had softened my view towards my own parents. Parenting was damn hard! It was easy to fumble even with the best of intentions. But I loved the heck out of him.

"Good, well give him our love."

"Sure will, Mom. Now listen, don't hide away; call me anytime."

Don't hide away? I was the one hiding. I had not told her I had changed residences and was now living with a roommate, someone I barely knew, a friend of a friend who had generously offered me a room in his house because I had nowhere else to be after leaving the house I shared with my partner, Sheri. Mom did not know that I was going through a body-numbing breakup with my loved one of many years. My guts were busted open and I kept it from her. I knew what she was going through but she did not know about me. I kept it all from her, the good times Sheri and I had, and now the bad.

I told myself that the pain of hearing me explain about this relationship would be too much for my mother. What I really meant was that the price was too high for me. I didn't feel that I had earned enough love back yet to squander any of it.

1995

MY FATHER DIED of cancer two years later. In a major reversal, I had come to love him deeply. Retirement had brought out a personable side to him. Always a silent presence, dependable yet remote, he now made more eye contact, even smiled, and seemed to be genuinely interested in people and things other than work. Gifted with a droll sense of humor that we used to have to dig out of him on long road trips, he more readily shared it. My mother was well known for her physical comedy (we called her Lucy), able to imitate any sound or dialect that came her way (this was both good and not so good in various situations) and the spectacle between the two of them was better than any TV comedy show.

I had also come to know my father as a person. When he had started to open up more, I understood that inside of him was a very young kid. He held on to childish resentments, squabbled over money, and walked about with a feeling of shame for his actions in his younger days. He wanted to be a good man, and he worried that he wasn't. "I hope I did okay" was something I would hear him say; then he would describe some way he thought he might have earned favor back from God. Although he and my mother never discussed this, we knew that he too was disowned by his strict Roman Catholic family—for falling in love with my mother while he was still married to another woman. Both women were pregnant at the same time. During one of our hospice visits he had said, "I hope I did right by marrying your mother. We tried to be decent and do the right thing."

On the day before his death, my sister and I stayed with him throughout the night. He was restless until the wee hours, tossing and turning. Towards morning he quieted down and we heard him say, "Well?" In unison we both replied, "Well?" After a long pause, he said, "Deep subject." My sister and I looked at each other with an amused but bewildered smile. Evidently his humor was still intact.

Despite all of this, I had not become the preferred one as I had hoped. In fact, I experienced a new kind of love story. For one, I became a family member again. I did what was asked of me in just the same way my siblings did what was asked of them. We took care of each other; we shared our sometimes fumbling selves; we cared for our parents.

The biggest part of the love story was seeing something that I had not understood before. And what was it? Nothing much to people who had it already, but just about everything to me: the quiet, easy devotion my mother and father had for each other— the way they held each other with their eyes—their trust that seemed to say *We will get through this, too.*

He died on my brother's birthday with only my mom by his side.

"Your good ol' daddy is gone," she said, when my siblings and I walked into the room. From this point on, stunned and grief-stricken, my mother became my preferred one.

Second Amends - Assisted Living - 2008

IT WAS A summer evening in Rock Island, and I was coming

back from an after-supper walk along the Mississippi River. It was a good walk, the humidity thick enough to make the air feel velvety just as the lightning bugs were coming out.

I loved that river. For years I was compelled by a yearning to return to it that nearly bordered on madness. I painted it, wrote odes to it, even made inquiries about moving back and living in a 19th century house in my old neighborhood just so I could see it every day. That deep, whirling, and muddy river reflected my hope and homesickness. At one point I would have done anything just to be asked to return, to be desired, called back to its banks.

Now, as I wiped the sweat from my face on my way back to my mother's assisted living apartment, I realized with a happy shrug that I loved the river and this hometown of mine in the same way I loved my life in Seattle. I belonged to both now. I had accepted an invitation. It didn't come in a frilly envelope written in a fancy script, nor was it procured from a revelatory vision in which God suddenly spoke to me in her thunderous voice. The invite came quietly, a few words at a time, and It said: *Life is good as it is. You are good as-is.*

As I put the key into the door of my mother's apartment, I noticed that the decorative placard she had placed on a nail near the keyhole contained the same scripture as the one on her refrigerator magnet. In jaunty script it read, "This is the day which the Lord hath made; We will rejoice and be glad in it."

Mom was sitting in her red recliner wearing the silky pajamas I gave her. She was waiting for the evening news to come on. She had just taken her bath and she smelled good, like Jergens lotion. It made me happy just to look at her. We had spent the last couple weeks of my visit talking like best girlfriends. Each night as I laid out the blankets and pillows on the living room floor where I slept, we would "gab," as she called it, until one of us yawned enough to let the other know it was time to go to bed. Then she would get up from her recliner, turn off the lights, and go to her room, snoring within ten minutes.

That evening, like many others, we told stories. This one was about the day I pointed the garden hose at anyone who tried to walk on the sidewalk in front of our house, young or old. I didn't remember doing it and I gently called her bluff.

"You were always a little booger, Nancy. I knew I was going to have to watch you every day of your life," she said, her eyebrows rising as she laughed.

"Yeah, I must have made your life hell, Mom," I said laughing, remembering all the telephone calls she had received from the school and from disgruntled neighbors.

I was an adventurous kid known as "the pill." More boyish than girlish, I took off on my bike with the neighborhood boys and talked them into doing crazy things. I dared them to ride their bikes into a carriage house (marked private) of a funeral home because I was sure there was a horse-drawn hearse in there with a dead body in it. I got them to throw dog-doo into a child molester's yard, and to do tricks like compete to see who could ride with no hands the longest without crashing. Later, as a teen, I worked hard to fly into my parents' faces on issues of integration, hippie-love, and opposition to the war. I barely understood the politics or history of those ideas, but I knew it was my job to yank their chain. I liked breaking rules.

"You were such a defiant rebel, Nancy. I do wonder what life would have been like if you had stayed here. Rock Island is pretty conservative," she showed me a thumbs down.

"I don't think I would have been able to, Mom."

I smiled a little trying to imagine living in my hometown as an artist, as a feminist, and as a woman who had spent much of her adult life identifying as queer. I think I would have been called worse than "the pill."

"I probably would have stayed a few years, then moved to Iowa City or Chicago, Mom. But life has its ways and I have my own ways …."

She smiled. "I suppose it does and I suppose you do."

I was not sure if she chose to understand me. We had a tacit "don't ask, don't tell" agreement when it came to my sexuality as well as my life as a painter. "She's a teacher," she often said to her church friends when referring to me, finding the term 'artist' a little bit too "out there" for her midwestern contingency. Maybe she described me as a spinster; I wasn't sure.

"Well, I am glad you are visiting now. I really miss you when you go back to Seattle." Her eyes filled with tears.

"You do?" I could feel she was telling the truth. There was a warmth in the room.

"You know I missed you so much all those years, Nancy."

"You did?"

"Oh, my Lord, yes. And Lisa, it just about broke her heart when you left. She cried for weeks and weeks."

"I didn't know that, Mom."

The memory of leaving my little sister behind on the train platform rushed into my mind vividly. I stayed steady on my feet and nodded.

"It was awful. And I worried so much about you. I wish I had known how to bring you back. I wish I had known what your life was like. You often said everything was okay but I knew it wasn't so great. And I was so dumb then I had no idea how to get on a plane by myself. I had no idea how to fly to Yakima when you had Nick. Daddy wouldn't have let me but I was also too scared to go on my own."

"Oh God, Mom. I missed you too, Mom."

My voice was shaking. I let it shake. *Let it be revealed,* I thought to myself.

"Nancy, we made a bad, bad decision. Our friends could not believe we let you go away like that. I was not strong then like I am now. I had no guts when it came to standing up to your dad. I wish I had been tougher and fought for you."

"Oh, Mom," I whispered. I felt a slipping in my gut. Something was going to come up.

"And Nance, you came out so good. Look at you! You raised Nick by yourself. However did you manage that?

How had I managed that? Through my many friends, my many angels.

"You went to college. How did you do that? Elma always says, 'That Nancy, she's tough as nails. She made something of herself.'"

"I guess I did okay," I said. "I had a lot of good luck along the way. I don't feel very tough."

I wasn't being overly modest. I stumbled on the roads that had opened for me and grimaced now at some of the detours I had followed. My life was not perfect and had never been, but it was A-OK. It was mine. I had faith in it, and in myself. And in truth, being forced to leave home had been a stroke of pretty good luck. It might have taken me years to go otherwise.

"Nancy, I'm sorry. Please forgive me. It is one of the biggest regrets of my life. I just have to get this off my chest." She wept quietly, looking into my eyes.

At that moment, I felt such love for her. For us. Nothing was going to fix that episode in our lives; I knew that. I still swallowed air when I thought about that summer in 1970. Yet, here we were in this room, holding onto each other by finally giving that time of sorrow a name.

Tears came into my own eyes and a very small girl's voice that cracked a little came out of my mouth. Suddenly I was standing there at the kitchen on Twenty-Third Street again and we were doing the dishes. I could feel it all.

"Mom," I said sobbing, "When you sent me away on that train, it hurt me so bad. It was the worst thing in my life. I have no words for the loneliness and sadness I felt losing you, losing Dad, everything. I still feel it. I wanted to come home, but I didn't know how. I felt so ashamed for so long even though I said I didn't. So, I just made my life there. I don't know how I made it either, but I did. Thank you for saying this, Mom. Thank you."

She looked at me a long time with those bright blue eyes of hers. Then she winked at me. I recognized it as the gesture of tenderness she gave to me as a child. It meant *you are mine.*

My Wonders of All - 2015 - Dementia

Tulips to my wonder of
all, my Wonders of all.
Of ALL - Tulips!!
My wonders
will always be there.
God was good to all.
The best!!

Margaret's last poem, 2015

AFTER I TOOK my mother for a ride in her wheelchair around
the memory center garden, after we had looked at and inside the
orange day lilies over and over and they were always new to her,

after we looked up at the Wisconsin prairie sky so primly blue with its five distinct white clouds, after I had pointed to them saying "look-it" because she loved to play "look-it," after she had said authoritatively, "Yes, those clouds are your boyfriends. You better pay attention to them," and after we belted out part of the refrain to her favorite Peggy Lee song:

Is that all there is?
If that's all there is, my friends, then let's keep dancing,
Let's break out the booze and have a ball.

After all that, we went inside to sit in her cheery little room. I sat in her big recliner provided by the center and she stayed in her wheelchair. She seemed sleepy and it looked like she had used up most of her energy on the garden tour. I wanted to keep her awake so we could have more time together that day.

"Let's sing some more songs, mom," I suggested. She nodded.

I gently took out her hearing aids and replaced them with the white earbuds connected to my phone so she could hear the songs she loved so much. Since the onset of her dementia, we spoke fewer sentences to each other and communicated more through singing. Along with Peggy Lee, she also loved Patti Page. Her favorite of Patti's was "In the Garden":

And he walks with me
And he talks with me
And he tells me I am his own.

She swayed, her eyes closed, humming. Her face was soft, a mildness in it that usually only the young have when they are being rocked to sleep. Then she opened her eyes and motioned for me to take the earbuds out. She wanted to talk. She took some time gathering her words, looking around her little room, then out the window. Her eyes squinted at something far away in the garden, then focused directly on me. Pushing herself upright in her wheelchair, she lifted her hand, wiggling two fragile fingers to get my attention.

"Daughter?" She had temporarily misplaced my name again. I was used to that.

"Daughter, I-I can't remember the name of the place where I am going, but I have my bags packed."

I knew she meant heaven. She talked about going there often these days. And always with her suitcase packed and ready. Sometimes she called out in the silence, "Angel? You there, angel? That you?"

"I've seen this place and it is so beautiful. I can't wait. I've got everything ready. My mother is there, and my father is there, and there are angels there waiting for me."

"I know, Mom," I said softly.

"Now listen … Daughter … Nancy, I have something to say. Don't interrupt me now, because I want to get it out," she said.

"I am really excited about going to this place. It is heaven, now I remember. I am so happy! But I am serious too. I don't want you or your sister to cry over me and I don't want you two to be sorry for me, okay? Because I am going to a beautiful place!" She made a wide circle with her hands, embracing the whole room. "I am happy about it. So do not worry. And all I want you girls to do is to wrap me up in some really, really pretty tissue paper (she pantomimed this part) and put me in a shiny box and let me go. Okay?"

It was clear what a gift she was giving us. How unafraid she was to go, how generously she was letting us go. I nodded yes.

"Good!" She said, announcing the end of the conversation by clapping her hands together once. She started to put the earbuds back into her ears but stopped short, looking at me strangely, her head cocked to one side. Her eyes were a soft blue. When I looked into them, they looked back at me. They were lucid eyes.

"And you ... you, Nancy," she said almost slyly, pointing her pinky at me. "I want you to become your real self. I want you to go out and have your real life. No more living in the shadows with me."

She tilted her head back, squinting her eyes, and smiling impishly.

"Daughter, go out and have yourself a ball."

NANCY KIEFER is a visual artist living in Seattle. An exhibiting painter, she spends part of her creative life writing poetry and short prose pieces. Nancy wishes to thank Ingrid Ricks for insisting she stay honest in this memoir and to the community at GenPRIDE for providing this connection and opportunity.

The Other Half of Transgender

BY M. AMES

" Is YOUR HUSBAND originally from Hawaii too?" In my stunned state, it took me a couple of minutes to realize what the proprietor of our bed-and-breakfast was asking. As it finally sank in, fear shook my core and I decided not to correct her. What would happen if she discovered Linda and I were two women? Our room is just a couple of steps away from her back door. Would the proprietor kick us out?

"No, they're from Virginia," I replied, carefully using nonspecific gender pronouns. This wasn't the first time someone had mistaken Linda for male. Matter of fact, it happens all the time. Linda's five-foot-ten stature, short-cropped hair, and the way she struts men's clothing give her a male persona at first glance.

I guess knowing how people perceive Linda, I shouldn't have

been surprised that the proprietor mistook her for my husband—yet I was. When this conversation ended, it took all the fortitude I had to walk away calmly. I had never been a major player in Linda's mistaken gender identity like this before.

Even inside our room, I felt we were still under the proprietor's watchful eye. Linda didn't look up; she was looking intently at her cellphone. I whispered so the proprietor wouldn't hear, "The woman from the B&B referred to you as my husband and I didn't correct her."

Linda came to attention. The words hung between us as my fear settled into the room. Linda's silence felt like a veil of protection as she took in what I had just said. Linda always thinks things through before speaking, responding calmly in situations that fluster me. To this day, I can't remember what Linda said. What I remember is that she comforted me, putting me at ease. I didn't understand how she could be so calm about the whole thing. I sure wasn't.

The morning after the incident, I got up early. I sat on the lanai at our B&B drinking my morning coffee and writing in my journal for a moment of peace. As I wrote, I took in the lanai setting with its wicker furniture, the tropical plants on the lawn, the smell of the trade winds that always blow in Kailua. It wasn't long before I noticed the proprietor walking around in her house just on the other side of the sliding glass doors. I got up and snuck into our room. Linda slept. I tried to read, but my mind fretted over yesterday's incident.

I thought about how people squeeze Linda and me into gender stereotypes. I the little woman; Linda the strong butch.

Did people see us the way the proprietor did? As man and wife? Linda and I fall in different places on the gender continuum, I know this, but we do see ourselves as equals. I'm wholeheartedly female, whereas Linda doesn't identify with either gender. This is where it gets confusing for me. Linda always talks about this with such confidence that I've concluded she's solid about her own gender definition or lack of. But lately she has started to describe her gender identity with less certainty. She's using the term 'transgender' more often and even wonders out loud what it would be like to take hormones. I can't tell how close she is, though. The more she talks about this, the more she seems to drift toward masculine appearances and behaviors. Her haircut gets shorter and more of her peers seem to be men. She's started to go to wife appreciation night with the guys. Where am I in all this? I don't know.

When Linda woke up, I suggested we go to the Vans Triple Crown surf competition in Haleiwa on the North Shore. Linda agreed. The long ride relieved some of our unsettled fears from the night before. Once on the beach, we lost ourselves in the cadence of the oncoming waves. I got engrossed in breaking down every move of the surfers, so familiar from my surfing days. Watching the waves, I recalled memories of the sea as if the sea were an old friend of mine. Linda sat next to me, engrossed too.

We explored Haleiwa after watching the surf competition. Haleiwa was a magical place for me when I lived there in 1970. It meant a lot to me that Linda wanted to explore Haleiwa too. Matsumoto's general store, a fixture of Haleiwa, still existed and was our first stop. He stocked a little bit of this and a little bit of that on his shelves. Matsumoto always greeted me like I was an old friend. This was the place to go in Haleiwa to buy a shaved ice. Pulling into the parking lot, I noticed a long line winding around the corner of a store I didn't recognize. We got in the line.

When it was our turn to order, the clerk asked Linda, "What flavor would you like, sir?"

"Lime," Linda answered.

I watched the look on the clerk's face as he realized he'd mistaken her for a man. Nothing was said about this between the two of them. This type of scene was familiar to Linda and me, and as usual nothing was said between us.

After Matsumoto's store, we decided to go to a quiet beach in Kailua. We didn't want to go back to the B&B. Lying next to each other on the beach, I realized the undeniable contrast between Linda's physique and mine. I'm six inches shorter than Linda to begin with. Linda always comments on how she loves my little hands. They're my mother's hands and my height is my mother's too. This might be what convinces people that Linda is male when she's around me. To add to the contrast, I like to fem up. Not too fem, but I like a nice ankle boot, with some tight jeans. If people don't out-and-out take Linda for a man when we're together, they at least do a double take.

I recall when I started referring to Linda as 'he' sometimes. She had just started talking about taking hormones and was sporting a more male persona. At first when I called her 'he,' I thought maybe I was just trying to get used to the changes Linda expressed, or maybe it was a way I was accepting Linda's appearance more. The incident at our B&B put a different perspective on this for me. I laid there trying to figure out what had changed because there are a lot of ways that Linda's always been male. A soft male. I call Linda this because of her quiet, high-pitched voice and her male persona. Even with this voice, she can command a situation in the same way a man does.

I've always pampered Linda's maleness or, as I've thought about it up until now, her "butchness." When she gets a haircut, I love to put my arms around her neck, rubbing my hands up and down, feeling the short hairs brushing the palm of my hand. I tell her how handsome she looks. She doesn't smell like a man, though; she has the sweet smell of a woman, and I love that about her. This is something we have in common. The question I ask myself lately is how far do I want her to go toward being male?

I look over at Linda on the beach and remember how her body has brought me such joy over the years. I know everything about that body. I have caressed it, explored it, and loved it. I know every wrinkle, wart, and hair, and am watching Linda's body age. I still want Linda in that way too. I wonder how much of Linda I would lose if she decided to take hormones. I've known women who have started taking hormones, and have observed them go through profound physical changes. Would I still want Linda in the same way if she transitions? It's not like she hasn't changed over the years. I've changed too.

If only I had someone to talk with about this. It doesn't help that I'm closeted about everything transgender that affects my life. With the transgender movement front and center in my queer community, I can't avoid talking about it. In these conversations,

I talk about transgender like it's out there somewhere and not in my life. I've been out as a lesbian for forty-plus years. Would I have to define myself as straight if Linda went through the change to a man? Would we be in a heterosexual relationship? I was entering foreign territory and not by choice, except the choice to be with Linda. Would I be ousted to the sidelines of my community if Linda were to go through the transition? Linda struggles with this and I know she already feels sidelined.

I feel anxious just thinking about being where Linda is heading. I keep reminding myself it's not my story to tell. Then I wonder, is it my story to tell? In thinking about this more, I realize that my story has been interwoven with Linda's story for almost forty years now. How do you take apart something woven together, woven over years and years of weaving? When I think of Linda's transgender struggles, I don't know how to pull out just my thread without unraveling the whole fabric. I'm surprised how tightly meshed we've become. Maybe this story has two main characters and I'm one of them.

Holding on to my anxiety, I am afraid to ask Linda specifics. This is where I'm left hanging. The incident at our B&B would have been a good segue way into a conversation, if only I'd had the guts to do it. I want to ask how serious she is about transitioning. I want to ask where I fit into her life if she does transition, but I am afraid. Afraid of losing the Linda I know and love. Afraid to tell my part of the story to Linda or to anyone—but I need to. How do I tell my story without outing my partner? I don't know.

Unfortunately, I wasn't able to sort any of this out in Hawaii. The gender incidents were mounting up throughout the trip—

one after another. Linda kept getting asked by someone in the women's restroom if she was in the right restroom, or told that she'd given them the wrong credit card because her female name didn't match what they saw. I just watched.

Close to our last day in Hawaii, I picked out a Korean BBQ place to go to at Pearl Ridge shopping mall. We walked in and sat down. The place looked like an old small roadside restaurant full of regulars. We ordered. The food was just as I remembered it. Linda liked it too. After finishing our meal, I walked up to the counter and asked, "Can I have the key to the restroom?"

They handed me the key as they explained, "The restrooms are located outside, around the corner." When I came back to the table, I handed the key to Linda. Our waitress, seeing this, ran across the restaurant with the key to the men's room, as everyone's eyes followed her. With the whole restaurant looking on, the waitress aggressively grabbed the women's key from Linda and handed her the men's key.

Linda in her soft voice said, "It's okay," as she grabbed the women's key from the waitress, handing back the men's key. Linda hadn't even come up with one of her witty comebacks. That's when I knew this public show of gender confusion made even her nervous. She looked lost.

"The restroom is just around the corner," I directed Linda.

Linda walked out the door to the restroom. I kept glancing around. Were people still staring at me? I couldn't shake the looks on people's faces when the waitress ran across the restaurant; those looks hung in my memory as if chained to me for eternity. I wanted to shrink into nothingness, slide out the door unnoticed, but instead I had to sit there. I wanted to go back to the world I lived in back home where we were accepted, a world we understood.

The waitress brought our check to the table, handing it to me even though it was Linda's credit card. I glared at the bill. How long does it take Linda to go to the bathroom? The waitress kept glancing over. Was she waiting for me to sign the bill? I decided to sign the charge slip even though it was in Linda's name. As soon as I signed the slip, the waitress noticed and walked over to retrieve it.

"Thank you," she managed to say, looking as embarrassed as I felt. I wondered if she too could hardly wait until we were gone. When Linda came back, we couldn't get out of there fast enough.

The Korean BBQ incident pushed Linda and me over the edge. I'd never before seen Linda express frustration like that when people mistook her for a man. Over the years I'd made a list of her witty comebacks. One of my favorites was "I'm in the right bathroom and I'm insulted you think I can't read." But Linda was speechless at the restaurant. Recently, when the gender-neutral restroom issue was making headlines back home, Linda proclaimed that she wasn't having as many problems in restrooms. I couldn't remember feeling tension like I was now when going into a restroom with Linda. It felt as if we'd gone back decades when gays stayed in the closet.

Linda has sometimes posed the question, "Why don't people just use non-gendered pronouns when they have doubts?" Linda shows me insights like this that I never think of. As much as I've talked to Linda about gender issues, I realize I still don't understand. In Linda's gender exploration, I always thought I was just a bystander. And maybe that's why I've also seen Linda's questioning as hers to explore, to self-identify, not mine. Now with this Hawaii experience I'm thinking I never really got it. As a feminine-looking woman, I don't have to process people's confusion about my gender; therefore I don't have the experience of people making comments directly at me about gender identity—at least not until the B&B incident.

Linda has expressed that she wants people to take her for who she is without having to use gender identity as part of that. That brought up a memory from a statistics class I took in the 80s. In the lesson, the instructor talked about gender stats by making a joke saying there are only two possibilities for gender and you would never add a category of 'other.' I have filled out forms recently where there are three categories for gender, but it's not common. If there were a legal gender category of 'other,' would the world accept Linda more? Would I—and the world—have more of an awareness?

Somehow, the incident at the restaurant made me realize I'd been thinking differently about Linda's gender identity for a while. Maybe it started when we got married and when I referred to Linda as my spouse people assumed I was talking about my husband. Or maybe it was years later when I saw the documentary "TransMilitary." There was a short interview in the film with a woman who had gone through the transition with her spouse who went from being her husband to being her wife. She talked about her fears of losing the person she'd fallen in love with. This woman's courage settled into my psyche and I go over and over those words like a broken record from time to time—and yet, I can't seem to talk about my own situation.

❧

THAT NIGHT BACK at the B&B Linda blurted out, "The proprietor may not be as prejudiced as you think." I could tell she was trying to reassure me.

"Why do you think that?" I asked her.

"She watches Ellen DeGeneres. She's got to have some idea about gays," Linda explained. I don't watch Ellen. I wondered how much she addresses trans issues on her show.

Linda googled "gay vacationing in Hawaii" to find something to do on our last day there. Her google search turned up list upon list of gay-friendly tourist spots.

Later that day, we walked around Waikiki. This was where Linda found more gay-friendly places than anywhere else. Late in the afternoon, we ventured into the Outrigger Hotel. Walking through the lobby, Linda turned to me, pointing over at the pool, and whispered, "Look at the gay men over there, lined up in their lawn chairs."

I glanced over at the pool, and seeing the gay men lined up sunbathing, I felt like I'd come home. On this trip I realized I was a tourist, not the local I'd once imagined myself to be. But here at the Outrigger were my people. They were Linda's people too.

We strolled into the bar, so grateful that no one stared at us. We sat down at a window table overlooking the beach. This sure was the place to soak up a tropical glow and relax.

We needed relief after the emotional roller coaster ever since the 'husband' incident. Linda ordered a fancy cocktail, I ordered a fruit smoothie, and we picked out some appetizers. Waikiki has always been a gathering place for all kinds of people. We called it the jungle in my youth. In this urban jungle, Linda and I could be among what we in the gay world call 'family.' Tomorrow we would be heading home and we were looking forward to it.

Back at the B&B that night, we got everything packed before going to bed. I was still processing the events here in Hawaii and I was pretty sure Linda was too. But we didn't talk about it that night. I just wanted us to enjoy each other. When we got into bed, I snuggled up to Linda, wrapping my body around hers, kissing her softly on the neck. She turned to face me.

"I love you," she said, as she pulled me closer. Now I could feel her soft, feminine body. "I love you too," I said.

<hr />

WHEN SHE came out in 1972, the gay rights movement was fresh and energetic and so was **M. Ames.** A couple of years later, she started journaling. Writing has soothed her over the years as well as getting her some journalism gigs. She has learned in recent years that coming out is a lifetime endeavor.

Ambulance Ride

BY KEVIN CHARLES PATZ

I WAS FLAT ON my back, my head propped up on a pillow, staring at the tail lights of cars in front of us as the ambulance rolled down I-5 from Northwest Hospital to Harborview Medical Center. It was a warm Seattle Thursday evening in July, but inside the darkened cabin I could feel a cool, air conditioned breeze circulating around me. I drifted in and out of consciousness, having been heavily sedated over the past several days. Somewhere amidst my foggy state, the phrase from the neurologist, "You may have a brain aneurysm" rattled in my head. For a brief second, I thought about the possibility my head would be opened up in the next few hours. Then the approaching lights of the city dimmed as I fell back into the sleepy state I'd been in for most of the past few days.

I woke up as I felt the ambulance pull up to the curb of the emergency entrance at Harborview. I slowly tilted my head up enough to see the double doors open as I was wheeled inside, suddenly drowned in fluorescent lighting. All I could see was the ceiling passing overhead. Then the medics wheeling me in became blurry and the sounds of moving gurneys and nurses' voices directing folks around became more and more muffled. Then nothing.

❧

ARRIVING HOME FROM my dealer five days before, I put out extra food for Marmalade, my orange tabby cat, in case I OD'd and it took a couple of days to find me. I considered Marmalade my guardian angel. I set out several bottles of Gatorade, because I really didn't want to die. Having lined up and readied my porn in front of the DVD player, I shot up a near quarter gram of crystal meth. I felt a rush of invincibility and a sense that everything was okay. At the same time, I felt as if my skull was shattering into a million small pieces. For a brief moment, I panicked, and then the sense of invincibility washed over any fear or caution and I was off to the races. The surge of energy propelled me into the living room, clumsily reaching for the remote control to turn on the DVD player loaded with porn. Then I was on the chat lines, looking for other like-minded tweakers. Frantically, I listened for the perfect phone sex partner, and before I knew it, hours had passed.

Then, a few hours—or days—later, I found myself at the baths looking to connect, to hold someone, and maybe more. Then the high began to wear off, but the headache remained and spoke louder and louder. I felt a stiffness in my neck and back. I went home and laid in bed hoping to finally fall asleep after three days, and hoping the headache would disappear. By the next day, I only felt worse. I was in so much pain that I forced myself to make the half-mile uphill walk to the nearest ER. As I walked through the sliding doors into the lobby, I debated whether to tell them I had recently been high. Once in the exam room, the nurse took my vital signs. I decided to level with her.

"I should tell you, I was using for several days, but I'm not high anymore." Her caring demeanor suddenly changed to one of indifference and aloofness. She directed me to lay on a gurney in the hallway. When I asked if they could move me into a room, she shot me an annoyed look.

"Well, that's not going to happen," she snapped as she brushed by.

I lay alone on the gurney for hours as medical staff passed by me as if I were invisible. I didn't feel like a patient to be cared for, but rather like trash, placed in their hallway waiting to be picked up.

"Aren't you going to run any tests?" I pleaded with a nurse who finally stopped to check on me.

"You don't need any tests ... you have back spasms due to your drug use," she said, and hurried away. Five hours after I arrived, they discharged me with a prescription for Percocet.

"You need to leave, Mr. Patz," the nurse sternly directed as she slapped a written prescription in my hand. "We don't want to have to call security."

Turning over on the gurney and feeling a rush of pain, I

tearfully implored, "Please don't make me leave! Aren't there tests you can do?"

"We don't want to call security," she repeated. To have to beg for medical care and be threatened was a depth of humiliation I hadn't before experienced. I slowly shuffled toward the sliding doors. It didn't seem to matter to them how, or even if, I made it home. Humiliation, shame, and rage collided with my physical pain. I felt beaten up, thrown to the ground and spat upon. I didn't want to be seen by anybody or look anyone in the eye.

I cautiously made my way to the bus stop, stiff as a board, feeling helpless, and hanging by a thread. After a stop at my pharmacy to pick up the Percocet, I finally approached my front door and collapsed onto my bed. I couldn't settle into a comfortable enough position to get even close to falling asleep. I tossed in one direction, and then turned in the other. Much of the day I spent staring at the ceiling as I noticed the shadows in my darkened bedroom shift, indicating the day was moving on without me. My neck and head felt heavier and heavier. In slow motion, I reached over to my bedside phone and called my primary care doctor.

"You need to go to the ER," she said. "I'll call to let them know you're on your way." I felt a mix of relief and gratitude. Her hospital, Northwest, was different from the one I had been at the previous night. My friend drove me to Northwest where, after a lumbar puncture and CT scan, they determined I had blood in my spinal fluid. I was immediately admitted and spent the next two days under heavy sedation. I was in and out of consciousness while the doctors pondered what to do next. Next turned out to be Harborview.

❧

I BEGAN TO hear sounds of people moving about, and then my eyes slowly opened and I realized there were nurses moving around on either side of me, adjusting tubes that seemed to be everywhere.

"Kevin, Kevin!" I heard a familiar voice plead for my attention. My mom and youngest sister, Mary, were staring down at me.

"Yes," I struggled to answer. Flat on my back, I labored to lift my head to look at them, and I had difficulty putting thoughts and words together.

"Your doctor called yesterday," Mom said. "We made the trip from Ohio and Minnesota overnight." Mom's eyes were red from crying.

I felt both embarrassed that I had disrupted their lives and grateful that they were at my side. Mom showed me a cartoon she drew of a sailor. The same as she used to draw me as a very young child. I was a young kid again and Mom was here to try to make things okay. She would ask me what I wanted to be when I grew up. I'd say a doctor or a teacher. I never said, Gee, wouldn't it be great to be a drug addict … better yet one who shot meth?

She looked so helpless. A wave of sadness surfaced through the fog. I slowly lifted my hand up to hold the cartoon and then handed it back. I managed enough energy to say "Thanks!" They reached down to hug me. I wanted to sit up and hug them, but was too confined by tubes and the meds. I placed my hand back on the bed and let the IV protruding from my arm settle by my side.

"Just get plenty of rest and we'll be back," my sister said, trying to sound upbeat.

"Okay," I replied. I stared back up at the fluorescent lights above me. I felt myself drift off as the tubes and nurses around me blurred and voices became muffled. Unconsciousness.

At some point during the next day, I was made aware that I didn't have an aneurysm, but probably had a subarachnoid brain hemorrhage. During my fleeting periods of consciousness, bits and pieces of the past several days continued to pass through my mind.

Then, on what turned out to be Sunday afternoon, I woke up again and Mom and my sister told me my heart had stopped earlier that morning. In hospital speak, I had "coded." In my sleepy state, I grasped at the fact that my life had just been saved. But there had been none of my life flashing before me.

"Did you see a bright light?" Mom inquired.

"No." Where was I during that drama, when firm hands were applying chest compressions in order to cease the flatlining? In my head I was trying to catch up to my own life. Surreal.

After about a week, I improved enough to be transferred to a regular room. It was tiny and painted a very relaxing aqua blue color. It had a view of downtown. At first I was relieved to be feeling better and be able to communicate. I was well taken care of by the nursing staff. But as I stayed there longer, the window view that at first I had enjoyed began to cause my stomach to tighten. I knew I would be released soon, and that view looked upon the real world where I would once again have to survive and try to make a fresh start.

How many other times had I had the same thoughts after a relapse? So many relapses over the past dozen years I couldn't even count them. But this time, I thought, had to be different. How could I even consider using again after almost dying? I couldn't put anyone who cared about me through this again. Yet, when I thought of returning to my small apartment, alone, my entire body turned into one big tight knot. All the other times I'd blown it; I felt like I had to put on a brave face for everyone. Oh my god, I thought. Of course I'll never go back out after this; I'd be crazy! It didn't occur to me to just admit part of me did actually feel a little crazy.

Going for short walks with the physical therapist served as one rude reminder of the constant obsessions I'd experienced for years whenever I'd go outside for a walk. On my walks around the hospital floor, I felt a twinge every time we approached any wastebasket. What if there was a discarded infant in one of them, I'd obsess. I couldn't resist looking. Then I felt compelled to circle back and check the wastebaskets again, inventing reasons for the physical therapist as to why I wanted to change our route. This was just a preview of the OCD that awaited me once out of the cocoon of the hospital. Not being confined to an ICU bed connected to tubes felt like a blessing when I was in the sanctuary of my hospital room. Venturing out into the world, even the short walks around my floor, set my heart racing and made my shoulder and neck muscles tighten. My obsessions were like bricks walling myself off from friends and family. I made jokes with visitors who commented on what a great attitude I had. I felt like I was two different people. Beyond this jokester they could see was a scared, anxious, obsessed boy crouched in the fetal position.

Ten days after I had arrived at Harborview by ambulance, aided by a cane on one side and my mom on the other, I slowly made my way back into the world. We had to make stops at the medical supply store and grocery store en route home. I wanted to keep riding around to avoid having to walk in the door of my apartment, but that obviously was not an option.

Back home, my ribs continued to be incredibly sore from having had CPR at Harborview. For the next month, every time I took a breath, stood up or sat down, reached for anything, or raised my body out of bed in the morning and lay down again at night to sleep, I was reminded of my brush with death and my promise that I would never put myself or family through that again. As the weeks passed and my ribs healed, I found myself able to once more do things that I used to take for granted. I was sleeping a little better. Finally I could raise and lower my arms without any sharp pain darting from my ribs.

My healing ribs, however, laid bare a raw loneliness. Not one person in my life really knew all of me. Some close friends weren't even aware of the events of recent weeks. They had become somewhat used to my vanishing act over the years. My sex and drug addiction was compartmentalized from everything else. There were my dealers and those I happened upon while high, and they were in a separate existence from those I considered my actual friends. But approaching my true friends became more and more difficult after my binges, and OCD only added to my isolation.

I fucking hated my life! The thought of telling people I had relapsed again made me cringe. I imagined the half hidden eye rolling of people in AA, the head tilts and sighs of well-meaning friends. My life wasn't supposed to be like this. I was supposed to have a career, be making decent money and not be on a merry-go-round to nowhere. Starting over and staying clean began to seem like a bridge too far. And with no more physical pain to remind me of August, it became tempting to forget. My sex drive started to return and I felt restless and antsy.

Soon, my apartment seemed smaller and the feeling of wanting to climb the walls alternated with recollections of how my mom and sister had looked at me so helplessly only weeks before. One evening as I lay on my bed, I tossed around, staring at the ceiling. The bedroom became my world. The shades were drawn. The white walls and ceiling were slowly creeping toward me, closing in. I felt more and more trapped. *What's the use?* I thought. I curled into a ball and my stomach felt tighter and tighter. Cramps followed, and then a strange kind of nausea. The sicker I felt, the less my mind seemed to grasp that there were alternatives to where my body and nerves were pointing me. I could hear the familiar voice telling me the only escape was to call my dealer—the same person who sold me the stuff that nearly killed me.

Still lying flat on my bed, I reached for the phone. I remembered his number and dialed it carefully as the stomach sickness I was feeling began to recede ever so slightly. A busy signal. Letting my head drop back to the pillow, I was now even more edgy. A growing irritability and impatience began to take hold, and then any possibility that I would abandon this mission disappeared. I would keep dialing until I got an answer, damn it to Hell! Then, finally, an answer. Relief replaced my impatience. Yes, he had some, and yes I could come over to pick it up in the next hour. He had changed addresses and was further away. A longer bus ride.

My hands shook as I tried to tie my shoelaces, failing several times. Impatience had returned. As I attempted to fit the key into the small hole to lock my apartment, my hands again trembled and I had to lean close into the keyhole to fit the key in, self-conscious that one of my neighbors would spot me. But I wouldn't be deterred. The ride on the bus was about three miles, but it might as well have been thirty. In the darkness, I strained my eyes to keep track of the streets we passed, panicking that I might miss my stop and get lost.

I felt mixed relief and anticipation as the bus pulled up to the stop and I found my way to Mike's apartment. We visited for a short time, during which I pretended to listen. Then I stared out at Lake Union and his words evaporated into midair. I put my cash out on his kitchen table waiting for him to produce the bag of dope. Goddamn it! I didn't come over for chitchat, I thought. At last! He opened the brown wooden box that contained what looked like a dozen small plastic bags with the white rocky powder.

Once he handed one of those to me, I quickly found a reason to leave and scurried to the bus stop. I spent the three-mile ride home fingering the bag in my pocket as if it might fall out or jump out onto the floor of the bus. Touching the bag offered reassurance. Jumping off the bus, I headed home, belching to the point of almost vomiting with anticipation of the rush.

In my apartment, I locked the door and checked it again. I hastily closed all the window blinds. I placed my porn in front of the DVD player. I put several days of cat food and water out for Marmalade. I frantically lined the powder on a plate and rolled up a dollar bill. *What am I doing?* I thought for a brief second as the powder burned its way up my nose. Desperation melted into relief. It was like July and August never happened. Again, I was off chasing my very first high.

Kevin Charles Patz, who was passionate about sharing his story with the world, passed away in March 2020 with his beloved mother, Rose, and sister, Mary, by his side. Having earned a Master's degree in Social Work, Kevin dedicated his life to helping others. He volunteered for the Lifelong AIDS Alliance, SeaTac International Airport, Washington Statewide Health Insurance Benefits Advisors (SHIBA), and Merrill Gardens, a senior facility. Kevin was honored with the HIV/AIDS Lifetime Service Award on World AIDS Day in 2017.

Time Capsule

BY NATALIE PASCALE BOISSEAU

I N MY SMALL blue car, I buckle my safety belt and back out of the driveway, out of the forest north of Seattle where I live. The GPS guides me toward the Ballard neighborhood in Seattle. There are forty-five minutes to make the trip to a café where fellow writers are meeting together. I usually feel happy and excited at the prospect of a writing moment shared with others. Not today.

A hard, firm mass is inside, blooming high in my chest at the base of my throat. It is familiar. The texture of loneliness. I wonder how to make it go away.

Growing up in the suburb of Montreal, I learned that Apollo landed on the moon as we were playing, my brothers and me, in our childhood backyard. My mother called us inside to watch the landing on the moon on a white and black television. We were excited. How could that be possible, a landing on the moon? As I am driving, I chase the memory from my mind, my windshield wipers chasing the rain away each half second.

The Pacific Northwest rain drops a curtain of waterfall on the car like an oil that penetrates all the cracks, my orifices, and seals me in. The loneliness in my chest tastes of salt and wraps me in the time capsule.

The traffic is slow, and the loneliness grows. I took the fastest road, but work crew after work crew signals me to stop. I wait; the rain is falling on their shiny bright yellow warning signs, the orange cones, the orange vests, odd citrus colors lost in the north of the Pacific coast. Patience, I tell myself. Patience, I tell the loneliness.

I drive south toward the locks of Ballard—the old town that has changed so much since I last came: tall, modern, urban Scandinavia with glass and sharp lines towers over small houses standing, last testament to Scandinavian migrants' old ways.

Shame now is entering with its wetness and humidity, a mold growing. I am ashamed that I cannot resolve the feeling. I am a grown woman who cannot buy her way into reasoning with the familiar loneliness. It feels so young, this knot caught in me, stubborn, with its head lowered, ignoring my attempts. I entice it, a pang in my stomach now, with a future cup of tea, saying *Look out around* during a stop. I also try distracting it. *See? There are other humans walking by; we are not alone.* Aloud, I add, "There is a life happening now at this minute." The knot tightens.

As I try to detach myself from it, turning the steering wheel, wanting to get away from it, the more it grips me, wants me to stay, and I feel a panic rising. It feels as a living presence, vibrating. I reason myself to more patience as I avoid potholes brimming with water, driving through the streets wet and shiny.

I want to scream and swear. One time I did swear at a therapist's office; I had let out a strong emotion swelling inside me. I swore, and the therapist interrupted me with her eyebrows lifted, disapproving. "Come on," she said to me. I am not allowed to swear, I know, as I swallow the feeling inside.

Stuck in my car, I engage the engine and navigate the city streets, driving as safely as the car runs smoothly. I am the one keeping us safe. How can I allow the living knot in my throat, the young voice rising in the present, without letting her take over? I shush her.

The more I try to escape it or to find ways to crack it, to resolve it, the more it hardens and becomes impenetrable. I should know that pushing or pulling on a knot will not release it.

In the childhood memory, there are pictures and drawings of the rocket returning to Earth's atmosphere. Its lost parts have detached and flown apart. For a moment suspended in time and space, the rocket has become the only home, waterproofed, airproofed, small.

I ask the knot, *What do you want from me?* It just wants to be, it responds. To be. *How can I help?* It does not want any help. It wants me sitting with it. Inside.

I am caught in the capsule now. A capsule where no one gets out.

In the capsule, there is a window. I am thirteen years old, sitting in front of the small window, in a corner, alone, my feet barely touching the ground. I am looking out at branches with green buds. The room is warm. People are talking loudly. I am alone in the immense forest of humans, sitting in the recess between two rooms. To the left there is a closed coffin. There are flowers near the casket. It smells flowery, but not L'Air du Temps, not my mother's perfume. Her scent is missing. It is an absence in the middle of the room, where there is a viewing for my mother's funeral, with a closed coffin. When they found her, it was already too late for an open coffin, I am told.

Finally we are driving down 15th Avenue, we, the she-knot and I, make our way through familiar sights of Ballard alternating with modern buildings. I feel a warmth spreading in me. *You see*, I tell the loneliness, *we are arriving soon, in a familiar and new place all together.* The humid air in the car is warmer, the car steams up.

Sitting in the recess between two rooms, I feel the warmth in my small chest. My throat loosens a bit. Tears start to fall, burning my skin. In the room to the right there are sofas with people milling around, and a large window lets in so much light. One woman, a friend of my mother, moves in my field of vision. She has seen me. She approaches me, moves me into her arms. My young body is docile. It moves into her embrace. I stop crying. My body holds its breath like a scared kitten stared at.

An energy arises. I need to do this alone, to cry alone, and now it is interrupted. The tear ducts shut. I do not know how to open up to my mother's friend. I do not know how to relax in her embrace. My mother's friend acknowledges me, sees me, my solitude, and my sadness. She overwhelms me with her awareness and I do not know how to be in my body again. The frail skeleton of grief, the lace of it, collapses inside of me.

She wants to console me with her motherly arms. These are not my mother's arms. My mother's arms and her embrace went missing weeks ago, before her death. I yearn for the mother to feel better. I wish for the mother to reassure me that she can care for her own sadness, her own capsule of loneliness. I want for her to drive safely through her own life, wishing for her lace of grief to not collapse. Loss does not have to tear us apart.

Maman, says the voice of the young self, sitting in front of the small window, in the recess between two rooms; *Maman, you did not have to go dying in the lasting snow of winter where all the layers of life are exposed, the pine needles fallen at different times of winter, the animals' traces. The grey smudges of melted dirt that reclaimed your being.*

I am with the young self, one with her invisible shadow. We are in the arms of my mother's friend. The young girl cannot cry. My mother's last living day is unspeakable. The tears are a trickle in the melting snow. Just a trickle that cannot be undone, growing in the middle of the funeral home, as I look at the branches and its buds through the window, through an opening between the arms of my mother's friend.

We are enveloped by the warm, round walls of the capsule flying through time. Will it burn entering the atmosphere? Will it fall in the water? Will it land on the earth gently, or will it come down crashing? The next moment is unknown and that is a very fearful moment that never ends. I am caught in the time capsule of my mother's last weeks, her last day, her last gathering with all those who loved her or had difficult relationships with her. Her capsule is made of utter, lonely solitude. Mine is right next to her, resisting the pull of her gravity.

The solitude is caught inside me. Inside the globe, its snow ashes shaking my chest when I approach too close. A warning and a fascination. Like a horror book you must hide before it threatens to devour you and drag you inside of it. I wrap my arms around this sphere to stifle its distress. At the same time, I tense my thin outstretched arms out to push away the dark energy menacing to engulf me.

The capsule walls off the grief, like a body's tuberculosis nodule walls off the bacteria, separating me from the young girl's grief, and from my mother's grief, lost inside my body for so long. But this wants to be seen, with finality, on this specific day as I am driving to Ballard.

I want my mother, not her distress, says the lump, the young girl in knots. *I was charged with saving her. I failed.* The knot unwinds softly. I, the driver, am letting myself feel this, letting the young girl tell me with unknown words her grief and her miserable sense of failed, impossible mission. I am one with the young one and the solitude she experiences in the suspended time.

There is only one parking slot available in front of the cafe. My body has helped us find our way. I unwind. I let the unknowing unwind on its own. We are together now in the ominous light of January. Sitting in the car, through the window, we see the café brimming with people. I don't have to do anything. Only feel her next to me. My body relaxes.

From a closed, static shape curled onto herself, inside me the young girl first moves gently, rolling from side to side, the walls of our capsule cracking softly. We are sitting in the middle of debris, feathers, torn blankets and torn book pages, dirty glasses and broken dishes, fragments of walls and panels falling around us. In the middle of her nest in disarray, she chooses me. Wet and moist she wants me as her quiet witness. I do not hug her. I do not talk.

As we watch through the car window, a young man gesticulates under the awning, in animated conversations with invisible friends, his backpack leaning on the concrete wall. I smile at him when he looks at me from the side, his gaze darting at me and the space next to me on the passenger seat.

I can either stay in the car and lose myself by entering the safe world of my marginal imagination or burst this capsule open, this enigma. The young girl leads. Trusting, I open the door. I look up at the milky grey sky. The rain falls on my face, the tears washed away.

NATALIE PASCALE BOISSEAU is writing a memoir on the suicide of her mother and the strangeness of healing, a novel, stories, personal essays and poems. She writes in French and in English. Natalie Pascale has published the story "Le Terrain Vague," at *Les Ecrits des Forges*, stories and poems in *Raven Chronicle*, and articles on the creative process of the Cirque du Soleil. She was awarded the *Best Specialized Articles* in Quebec in 1990 on First Native Social and Legal Issues. Weaving in contemplative arts, she facilitates the workshop "The Writing Practice."

Everything and Nothing: A Phone Message

BY MARY EDWARDS

MY DOCTOR'S VOICEMAIL said everything and nothing. I froze when I heard it. "Hi Mary. This is Dr. McCandless. I need to talk with you so please call back as soon as you get this message."

I'd had a brain scan the Friday before and I figured if she had good news she would have left it on voicemail. I hadn't been worried. Now I was.

I breathed shallowly, holding my body still and quiet like I always did when I wanted to control my emotions. The red couches beside me sat quietly too. The breeze outside even settled and our raspberry plants didn't move. Perhaps if my world and I were still, the universe wouldn't notice us and nothing bad would happen.

I returned the phone to its cradle and stepped softly from our den into the kitchen to tell my partner, Ann. Before I spoke, I leaned against the door frame trying to imagine how this phone call could fit into spring break. It couldn't.

"Ann," I whispered, my throat too constricted to speak any louder.

She looked up from washing dishes and I shared the doctor's message. Her eyebrows lifted and her body straightened. "That doesn't sound good," she said, keeping her voice even. "You should call her back."

Ann had been with me ten years before when I'd lost control of my limbs and had begun projectile vomiting after waterskiing on a lake south of Seattle. We'd gone to the area's small emergency room where the young doctor did lots of tests that didn't explain my troubles. In the past weeks, Ann had seen my increasing fatigue and knew there was reason for concern.

"I don't want to mess up our break," I said. "So no. I won't call. Not yet. I'll call Monday when we're back at work." Ann pursed her lips and nodded. She knew I was stubborn and wouldn't call until I was ready.

I had always assumed there was nothing wrong until evidence proved otherwise, but experiences over the last couple of weeks concerned me. I'd been so weary that I hadn't had enough energy to grade my students' writing, clean my classroom, or even walk unless it was absolutely necessary. Mornings I hadn't gone to the gym like I usually did, and I barely got to school before my students. Once I'd been so fatigued that for the first time in my seventeen-year teaching career, I hadn't prepared the day's lessons. Unaccustomed to being unprepared, my head and hands jittered with panic, and I ran next door to borrow another teacher's lesson.

I raced back to my room to read the lesson and prepare for class. As I organized the chairs, the floor seemed to swing upward. My face felt cool and my lips tingled, so I-sat. I had experienced these spells since junior high school when the basketball team had nicknamed me "Casper" because I got so pale. But the faintness was now occurring more often.

Ten minutes after sitting, my head cleared and the bell rang. I stood to greet my students, who came in like bumper cars bouncing boisterously off one another. For them this was a typical day. For me it was not. The faintness abated, and I taught my classes as though nothing were wrong, but a shadow darkened my day. What had happened?

This phone message confirmed my fears that what had happened was serious. I thought of other troubling experiences. Over the weekend my vision had doubled when Ann and I biked to a favorite destination, Redhook Brewery, in a nearby town. As we coasted downhill, I saw two Anns. Two speed limit signs. Two crosswalks. Two of everything. I closed one eye, returning to singular vision. Problem solved, I thought.

When we reached the pub two hours later, I told Ann my world had twinned and described my clever solution. She was neither impressed nor amused.

"You need to email the doctor," she said, putting down her fork and no longer chewing. You've got to be kidding me, I thought. I was exasperated. She knew I'd been seeing the doctor more often than usual that year and found the appointments frustrating. "She'll just tell me to drink more water," I said.

After forty-three years, a lifetime of symptoms no doctor could explain, I was accustomed to living with my oddities. Doctors doubted there was anything wrong, and I doubted myself. I figured maybe everyone dealt with symptoms they didn't talk about and these were mine.

Over the years I'd generally seen a doctor only for routine exams, but this year I had seen Dr. McCandless so often I felt like a hypochondriac. I had made appointments about headaches, swaying, blurred vision, dizziness, balance issues, and vertigo. She always told me to drink more water.

Setting her Longhammer IPA on its coaster, Ann was unusually stern. "Put all of the symptoms in one email," she told me.

"Okay," I relented, "I'll email the doctor, but I'm not going to drink more water."

I scheduled an appointment with Dr. McCandless for Friday. When she came into the exam room, her jaw was set, and she was serious. "Tell me about your double vision," she said. I described the bike ride and experiences in my classroom. Still frowning, she said, "I think it's time for a CAT scan."

The idea of having a CAT scan didn't bother me. I figured it was a rule-out. I believed I had diabetes. All my life I had reacted strongly to sugar, sinking into a deep sleep after a Coke or candy bar, so diabetes seemed like the obvious cause.

I spent the weekend feeling relieved that after decades of dizziness and blackouts someone was taking my symptoms seriously. But since my doctor's voicemail, I no longer felt relieved. My body stiffened and my stomach felt queasy like it did after I fainted. I thought this must be bad news.

I spent the week trying not to think about the call. Ann and I took long walks around our neighborhood, breathing in *Daphne odora's* light perfumes and admiring azaleas blooming in a splendor of magentas, purples and whites. We weeded our raised vegetable beds, and I pruned the roses. We hiked where winter's snows had melted. We did not discuss my doctor's daily messages. Refusing to acknowledge my fears, I felt wooden, like the dead rose branches I'd pruned.

Dr. McCandless called every day that week. On Thursday, she left her home phone number. A really bad sign. I still didn't call.

The last day of our break that week, Ann and I spent the afternoon at a women's spa. When we checked in, an attendant handed us robes and shower caps. She also told us how to prepare for our scrubs, the day's most decadent delight.

After lounging in the heated rooms, we traveled to the hot tubs where I noticed women with all kinds of bodies: women scarred from surgeries, obese women whose abdomens swayed side to side, and skinny women whose muscles flexed. As I took in their bodies, I wondered, "Would the doctor's calls mean my body would change?"

Determined to think about something else, I imagined my mom in this spa. She could not abide this place. When she's making a strong statement, she asserts that she cannot "abide" something. Southern women do not say "hate," and they do not lounge naked in hot tubs with other naked women—even if everyone is wearing a shower cap. Ann and I chatted casually as we soaked. We didn't talk about the unreturned phone calls.

When we had been in the tubs for half an hour, two women called our numbers and directed us to lie on pallets. A line of pink butts had preceded us into the scrub room. We lay face down and the scrubbing began. The women doused us with buckets of warm water and then scrubbed every bit of us with a coarse soapy pad. After the scrub I heard one newcomer say to her friend, "That was ... thorough." Yes, it was; nooks and crannies were now exfoliated. Afterward, we ladled water from the spa's slimy, green mugwort trough on each other's bodies. The water was soothing, like cream on a sunburn. For that moment, I pushed my fears deep and relaxed.

Back home with soft skin, I made cosmopolitans and crackers with goat cheese and grapes to eat on the deck while Ann grilled salmon and peaches. I was determined that we would enjoy the last moments before we returned to work and I got my doctor's news. Because it was a warm day in Seattle, we wore T-shirts. Mine had an image of a Day of the Dead woman's skeleton wearing a hat with a flower for flourish. Underneath the image was the restaurant's name, "Frida's, Antigua, Guatemala." Ann's shirt was light pink with the soft white image of a glass of milk. The inscription underneath read "half full." That's how we saw our lives. No matter what this unreturned phone call meant, we knew our glasses were half full and our lives were full.

As the sun dipped over the city to the west, the air chilled but we ignored our goosebumps for the moment. The setting sun's slicing rays glinted off Ann's glasses as she turned to me. Her dimples creased, and she took my hand. "I love our friends and family," she said, "but my favorite times are when it's just you and me sharing a simple moment on the deck."

I held Ann's soft hand in mine and scanned our backyard. It was early spring, so leaves were just beginning to sprout on the grape arbor. Along the path, tulip leaves bounced in the breeze, their red ends looking like paintbrushes. Soft pink flowers the color of Ann's shirt covered the camellia. Spring scented the air.

"These moments are my favorites too," I said to her, taking in the setting sun's pinks and oranges. I looked back at her, lovely like the sky, and was silent for a heartbeat. "These moments are my favorites too," I said again. For this moment, I wasn't even thinking about the phone calls.

After school ended the next day, I went to the principal's office for privacy and finally called Dr. McCandless. When she and I connected, she said, "I'd guess you already know this is going to be bad news." I did, and it was. "The CAT scan revealed a brain tumor that will need to be removed surgically as soon as possible."

I had never been one to panic and I didn't now. As she talked, I looked around. Books like *Why Are All the Black Kids Sitting Together in the Cafeteria?*, *The Courage to Teach*, and *I, Rigaberta Menchu* crowded the shelves. I'd also read those books, staples for progressive educators.

After my doctor delivered her news, she asked if I understood. I did—partly. I didn't yet know what this tumor meant for me, and I was calm. When Dr. McCandless invited me to ask questions, I asked about an upcoming opportunity.

"I'm supposed to go to Santa Fe in a couple of weeks as part of a state team on writing assessment. Will I be able to go?" For a moment she was silent, and I wondered if she had heard me. Then she spoke.

"In two weeks? No. You cannot go. Do you think you're in shock?"

I didn't think I was in shock. I had never reacted with strong emotion to bad news, so my calmness didn't feel odd. Also, I'd never had brain surgery before. I thought of this diagnosis like previous ones. When I'd had strep throat, I had just figured out what I could do then and what needed to wait until after I healed. I supposed neurosurgery would be like that.

"You've been assigned a neurosurgeon," she continued, interrupting my thoughts. "He's done some of those videos of brain surgeries. He's impressive, a renaissance man. You'll like him. Make an appointment with him as soon as possible." Having an impressive renaissance man as my surgeon sounded great.

I hung up and called Ann on my flip phone.

"Are you sitting down?" She was.

"I just got off the phone with Dr. McCandless. I have a brain tumor." Ann was quiet as I told her everything I knew, which wasn't much. "I won't be able to go to Santa Fe," I said.

"Yes, I figured that." She didn't cry. She didn't ask questions. In fact, she hardly made a sound. Neither of us knew yet what this diagnosis would mean for my life—for our lives.

"Are you okay?" I asked. She said she was. "We'll talk more when we get home."

"Yes," she said. "I love you."

"I love you, too."

I sat for a moment, enjoying the quiet. This office felt like a sanctuary, and I thought about so many meetings I'd had here. Sometimes I had come here to argue with the principal, or to tell him what a great job he was doing. Other times I had come here for help. I knew I'd have to deal with my news when I left this space, but for the moment I enjoyed the quiet. I wasn't yet ready to deal emotionally with this tumor. I wasn't in control of my future, but for now I was in charge of this space.

"I have a brain tumor," I said aloud to the books. That sounded melodramatic, but the books stayed calm. At last I opened the door and walked across the hall to tell the counselor I wouldn't be able to proctor the state exams. Not following through on a responsibility was unusual for me, so she tilted her head like a confused puppy.

"Are you okay?" she asked, and both of us were quiet. With her concern, something in me shifted. I felt a small crack as my situation's gravity shook me. A single tear slipped from my eye.

"I have a brain tumor."

MARY EDWARDS lives in Seattle, Washington, with her wife Ann, her muse for 25 years, and their dog Dosewallips, who teaches them to live in the present. Mary's memoir, *Recalculating: Finding New Routes at Life's Detours*, describes how coming out strengthened her, helping her live powerfully after brain tumors. *(Photo credit to Jack Straw Productions 2016).*

What Do You Want?

BY HOPE BLESS

"WHAT DO YOU want for your birthday?" This is the all-important question. I'm lying down on the sofa hooked up to the oxygen, which sounds like a WWII aircraft going down, trying to get more comfortable without asking for help. I am not well. I have not been well for several years. It seems to me that this fixation on the question, "What do you want for your birthday?" is intricately entwined with terror that it might be my last. But while others flutter about me in a state of panic, it is all I can do to get down a little broth and try not to sabotage the latest medical intervention. Another part of me weighs what I have been through in the past against this latest thing and thinks it isn't nearly as scary in terms of life and death. I also feel like it is my job to put a brave face on things to ease the suffering they are going through but feel they have no right to share. The last two b-days came and went without my knowledge as I fought for my life in two six-month comas that struck me down on consecutive December 23rds, ruining my best friend Liz's birthday.

No one saw the illness coming. I was just thirty-seven years old and in peak fitness—climbing, running, cycling, swimming, and lifting six days a week with longer weekend big-wall climbing and the occasional triathlon or century ride thrown in for fun. Getting a good sweat on and creative problem solving while climbing were types of meditation for me that depleted excess physical energy and left my mind free to explore solutions in the studio later in the day with a calm, focused mind. But on the morning of December 23 my 'wasbund' Jim thought I looked a little funnier than usual and took the day off to drag me to my doc kicking and screaming. Once there I began the usual clowning and sarcastic one-upping with the staff that left us wiping away tears of laughter and grabbing our sides. 'Twas the season to be jolly. Jim was thoroughly disgusted and giving me that "this is so inappropriate" look and the doc was wrapping things up and slapping me on the back when my blood pressure dropped to fifty over thirty and kept dropping as I crumpled to the floor in an undignified, unconscious heap. I remember looking up and trying to grab the arms trying to catch me that were at once so close and so impossibly far away—and then there was nothing at all. The rest was told to me many months later in bits and pieces as the doctors determined I could handle.

In the ambulance to the hospital, the paramedics were losing the battle for breath but managed to sustain me, calling ahead instructions for the ER docs to be ready to perform an emergency tracheotomy, get me hooked up to life support, and then park my carcass in the last ICU bed available in the city. All vital organs were failing at once, but being in the coma allowed my body to battle with death.

During the first few months, Jim would get calls at all hours of the day and night to rush to my side for final farewells. They only had to use the hospital intercom because Jim spent all his time there. Much of the time, though, he was not allowed to be by my side so the staff could do all they needed to with speed and precision. Having just moved to the area for work and knowing no one, Jim spent his time wandering hospital corridors and curling up in corners of empty hospital rooms to weep in the darkness, utterly alone. It is hard to comprehend all this very private man suffered.

The doctors never discovered what caused the sudden system failure. Whatever the initial attack on my immune system, the illness resolved itself into ARDS: Adult Respiratory Distress Syndrome, which has a 50 percent survival rate.

Coming out of the fog, all sorts of irrational thoughts crossed my mind. I perceived many threats that for the most part were not real, probably because the actual threats to my survival were still very present dangers. I remember getting mad at Nasty Nurse (there's always one) when I was coming out of the first coma. She liked to hold my voice box hostage as I was being weaned off the respirator for a few lucid moments at a time.

"You will not survive this unscathed," she said, quite matter-of-factly, whenever she had the opportunity to pontificate and spread good cheer. This kind of thing gets my undies in a bunch and I went into a wee rage, albeit a steaming silent one; remember, Nasty Nurse still had possession of my voice. Nevertheless, I managed to get enough emergency alarms going to get the entire medical team to my room within minutes. When she relinquished my voice box with a dramatic eye roll, I demanded she be removed from my team immediately and for the duration of my time in the ICU. Mind you, while I railed against her, my right side was still partially paralyzed, which was an inconvenient fact supporting her thesis. But it only served to fuel my self-righteous indignation that came out in weak, wispy whimpers spaced one word at a time with the staff filling in the words by guessing at my ever-so-slightly crazed meaning—a towering inferno of inarticulate squawking sounds. On that front not much has changed.

Now, I concede she had a point. Okay, okay; she was right. (I hope that makes her happy.) I began to discover my recovery was not going to be all the roses and rainbows I had envisioned. I had already been knocked down many times in my young life and I always popped right back up like a wind-up toy ready to rock and roll. I had contracted polio from the vaccine when I was two years old. This resulted in many corrective surgeries that I took in stride. Even after my leg was amputated in my thirties, it was always the same. Once knocked down I pop tarted up like a party trick performed by rote. But this … this was different. It was not so much pretty rainbows as a rain of blows, each more staggering than the last. For every minuscule gain, I got sucker-punched with sweet nothings like strokes and grand mal seizures, life threatening infections, and emergency surgeries like this latest intestinal skirmish where my guts decided to spontaneously combust by tying themselves in knots as if they could get an NEA grant for experimental peritoneal art. Or intestinal tatting. To what end?—as I lay bleeding out on the table due to life-saving emergency surgery while on blood thinners for the chronic clots in my arms and legs from the months and months of immobility, and from the destruction that happens with sepsis. My life ever after surviving these things was not defined by having what I wanted; it was best handled by assessing what was my reality in the moment and finding a way to accept it without accepting defeat.

But on *this* night I am alive and it is my birthday and all my friends want to know is what I want for my birthday. It's not the easiest question for someone in my circumstances to consider, but I'm usually game for anything and I know they mean well.

Looking at their sweet faces, I am trying very hard to smile and pretend to enjoy the music and everything, but all I can think about is the likelihood of this shitbag attached to my stomach sliding off or leaking on the new dress Liz gave me. If I tell the truth, though, the emergency colostomy was already this year's gift—I didn't even code.

Come on girl. You have to think of something – anything – it's your day. I wipe the sweat from my face, still with this ear-wide grin, which is beginning to hurt, and try to think it through. But it's so exhausting to stay conscious that organized thought seems a herculean task. *What do I want for my birthday?* I can't wrestle synapses to sense.

My friends seem excited but their eyes are a little wild. I can't tell if they're afraid I'm going to die before we get the matter settled or if they're angry because I fucked up the last few birthdays. I struggle up to a seated position and scoot over into my electric wheelchair. Saying I need a little air might frighten people, so I just make my way to the front door. Though it is a cold night in January, something draws me there. The night is so very still, the sky like blue-black velvet with very few stars. It is so beautiful it nearly entices me to just disappear into it and roll on out.

"What do you want for your birthday?"

Since my birthday comes just ten days after Christmas, for most of my life it has been almost hyperactively ignored. My parents were notoriously bad budgeters, so by Christmas Day they had already gone further into debt than they realized or were ready to admit. When talk turned to my birthday, as it inevitably did in the days that followed, my mother would dart around corners combining the clanging of her cleaning supplies with sighs so searing they brought to mind the crucified Christ's last breaths. Crazy as it was, the clanging and crucified sighs hit their mark. The effect was always the same: our collective jaws snapped shut, I retreated into guilty silence for having been born, and my brothers pretended I didn't exist. She was a crack shot in the guilt game. There wasn't a lot to do. School was out for a few weeks; the weather was cold and wet. We were bored and our well-practiced protocol for that was to start a fight.

Now, with all this emphasis on asking what I want for my birthday, I am itching for a real blowout to break up the single-minded purpose of these people who love me and have gathered to celebrate me. I wish they would just let me be. It's a bad habit of mine, but I've always rather enjoyed being less important than my brothers and out of my parents' field of vision. As I've grown older, this has extended to my friends, and it has felt almost like a necessity to be out of the spotlight. Even when hosting a party or being the focus of one, I have found ways to escape. Solo walks in the early morning hours when the party is raging. Locking myself into my studio to contemplate a composition or just to inhale the smell of oil paint and lose myself in a dreamland of color and texture and ideas.

"What are you doing?! Come inside!"

Reluctantly, I leave this still, quiet place and return to the party.

"Sooo...What do you want for your birthday?"

On the stereo, Dar Williams is singing one of my favorites, "When I Was a Boy." I remember days like those. Coming inside, I stop beside the altar Jim built for things that remind me that love, joy, peace, and truth are the real treasures in this transient life we are given. My eye lands on the little white box my hand always reaches for. When Lori gave me this, she scrawled in pencil on the top, 'A little breath of Colorado.' The writing has long since faded, but my fingers find the imprint of her hand. Inside the box is a fragile little leaf. Of all the gifts I have been given, this is the one that I keep coming back to. It always makes me pause and smile, take a deep breath, and find I am home.

The other important gift that was given to me was a gesture of kindness that had such an impact on me it is hard to explain, and so I've kept it in my heart. It was when I was being weaned off the respirator after coming out of my first coma. I still thought Christmas was coming in two days and kept getting confused about the time lapse. Jim had talked the doctors into allowing him to take me out of the hospital for a few minutes to let me feel the sun on my face and see the flowers so I could understand we were well into the end of spring and nearly ready for the summer solstice. With a team of grim-faced ICU staff a few steps behind us, he wheeled me outside. At once the air was warm and balmy, filled with the scent of green growth. I could smell the rich soil, feel that sun warm me within and without, hear the birds singing in the trees. At first it was almost too much. I kept my eyes closed to let each sensation flood my senses. When I opened them, tears streaming down my face and a huge smile breaking out all over, I had to blink away the blurry tears so I could take in each exquisite sight. Flowers that had just pushed their way up from the dark into the light. Even a few poppies that somehow found the strength to break through the asphalt of the wheelchair path, determined to bloom. The music of the lacy leaves in the trees along the way took my breath away and infused me with life itself.

"What do I want for my birthday? What. Do. I. Want. For. My. Birthday?"

My voice is so weak it takes enormous effort just to form the words. Jim brings more blankets and now they are all just looking at me. Waiting.

The tears start rolling down and won't stop. At last I whisper, "What do I want for my birthday?" After another sweet breath

I say, "Birthday is gift. Some never get one. It is in every breath. Birthday is gift."

HOPE BLESS is a one-legged woman who is otherwise unremarkable in every way. She did not so much grow up as get yanked up from among the "good kids" and placed permanently on the prayer list and forced scripture until she fled from whence she came and found her place among other societal rejects where she found the courage to be as queerly quirky as she was born to be.

Acknowledgments

THIS ANTHOLOGY, BRAINCHILD of writing coach Ingrid Ricks, was a labor of love. Her passion for the power of story is evident within minutes of meeting her. Ingrid was the spark that ignited this special collection of personal narrative essays. GenPRIDE invited Ingrid to conduct a four-week writing intensive, but the participants were eager for more. Monthly workshops ensued and a cohesive group of diligent writers took form. Ingrid's expertise with authoring her own personal narratives motivated and inspired the writers to dig deeply into their own lives. As the group shared with each other by writing of profound experiences they had long guarded, the bonding that occurred among them was life-changing. For all this, Ingrid was the special ingredient, offering ongoing advice, encouragement, and support.

Beyond the tremendous undertaking of the writing itself, the participants graciously contributed to the work of publishing this anthology. Special thanks to Irene Calvo, who offered her editing skills, Amy Rubin, who produced the recordings for the audio version, and vocal coach Alyssa Keene from the Jack Straw Cultural Center who supported the authors in their audio recordings.

Lastly, we appreciate those who provided funding to make this book possible: Nordstrom, Inc.; the City of Seattle Aging and Disability Services; and the King County Veterans, Senior, and Human Services Levy.

About GenPRIDE

ESTABLISHED IN 2015 in Seattle, Washington, GenPRIDE is a nonprofit organization focused on the health and well-being of older LGBTQIA adults throughout the region. We are committed to providing them with a safe place to come together for education and recreation, to exercise, and to socialize. In addition, we conduct training sessions for housing and healthcare providers on how to create a more welcoming and inclusive environment for LGBTQIA seniors.

The writing workshop that gave rise to this anthology is just one of our activities that build connections. Our programs are varied and foster meaningful ties among midlife, older, and younger generations of LGBTQIA people in our community.

The need for a space to come together has become even more evident in light of COVID-19—most everyone now understands what it is like to be isolated. We have built substantive relationships with other organizations to undertake the construction of a new LGBTQIA senior community center on Seattle's Capitol Hill by 2022. GenPRIDE has been given an extraordinary opportunity to own this space for generations to come. The center will be co-located on the ground floor of a new affordable housing building for LGBTQIA seniors, a first of its kind in Washington.

Once we can safely gather again, GenPRIDE will re-open a physical location that will continue to provide dynamic connections and interactive opportunities for Seattle and King County's LGBTQIA seniors and their supporters.

Please join us at www.genprideseattle.org to learn more.